NEW MERM

D0661635

General Editors:
William C. Carroll, Boston University
Brian Gibbons, University of Münster
Tiffany Stern, University of Oxford

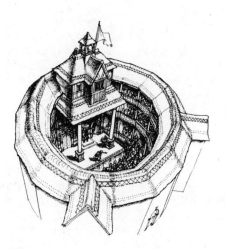

Reconstruction of an Elizabethan Theatre
by C. Walter Hodges

NEW MERMAIDS

NEW MERMAIDS

JOHN WEBSTER

THE DUCHESS OF MALFI

Edited by Brian Gibbons
Fifth Edition

methuen | drama

LONDON • NEW YORK • OXFORD • NEW DELHI • SYDNEY

METHUEN DRAMA
Bloomsbury Publishing Plc
50 Bedford Square, London, WC1B 3DP, UK

BLOOMSBURY, METHUEN DRAMA and the Methuen Drama logo are trademarks of
Bloomsbury Publishing Plc

This Fifth Edition first published 2014
Reprinted 2015 (three times), 2016 (four times), 2017, 2018

First New Mermaid edition 1964
Second Edition 1983 © Ernest Benn Ltd 1964, 1983
Third Edition 1993 © A&C Black Ltd
Fourth Edition 2001 © Bloomsbury Publishing

© Bloomsbury Publishing Plc 2014

A catalogue record for this book is available from the British Library.

ISBN: PB: 978-1-4725-2065-4
ePDF: 978-1-4725-7183-0
ePub: 978-1-4725-7159-5

A catalog record for this book is available from the Library of Congress.

Series: New Mermaids

Typeset by Country Setting, Kingsdown, Kent CT14 8ES
Printed and bound in India

To find out more about our authors and books visit www.bloomsbury.com
and sign up for our newsletters.

CONTENTS

ACKNOWLEDGEMENTS

For support of various kinds I am very grateful to Andrew Gurr, David Lindley, Hermann Real, and Jane Saunders, the Brotherton Librarian at the University of Leeds. At the New Mermaids many thanks to Tiffany Stern, my General Editor, and to Simon Trussler, who set the text with calm precision and excellent judgement.

BRIAN GIBBONS
October 2013

INTRODUCTION

Plot Summary

The Duchess of Malfi is a widow, but still young. Her two brothers – Ferdinand, who is her twin, and the Cardinal – visit her in Malfi. The Duchess chooses Antonio, a gentleman newly returned from France, as her steward. She appoints Bosola, a discontented soldier who has served the Cardinal, as her Master of Horse. On departure the brothers warn her to remain chaste and unmarried but the Duchess secretly woos and marries Antonio with her waiting-woman Cariola as witness.

Almost a year passes.

The birth of her first child is an event which Bosola discovers and reports to the brothers without discovering either the father's identity or the marriage. Ferdinand reacts with violent passion and vows revenge; the Cardinal displays rage too, but his is cold (II.v).

A gap of two to three years.

The Duchess has had two more children in secret; Ferdinand arrives at her court and visits the Duchess by night to extort a confession. As she prepares happily for bed Ferdinand appears, gives her a dagger with the words 'Die then quickly' (III.ii.70), threatens her unseen lover with death, and disappears again into the dark. The Duchess decides Antonio must leave at once for Ancona, explaining this as his dismissal for false steward-ship. She tells Bosola that Antonio is her husband: Bosola tells Ferdinand. She sends Antonio with their eldest son to Milan, but is herself arrested by masked men and taken with her children to Malfi.

Ferdinand visits the Duchess by night. He gives her a dead man's hand. Then Bosola draws a curtain to show her children and husband dead. A group of madmen further distress the Duchess. Bosola, now disguised as an old man, shows her presents from her brothers: a coffin, cords and a bell. The Duchess prays, kneels, and is strangled. Her children are put to death. Cariola sees the body of the Duchess and reacts in terror. She is strangled. Ferdinand views the body of the Duchess. He shows signs of incipient madness and lycanthropia (believing he is a wolf), refuses to reward Bosola, and leaves. The Duchess stirs, speaks again and finally dies.

Ferdinand goes mad. Julia, the Cardinal's mistress, seduces Bosola but dies kissing the Cardinal's poisoned book. Bosola overhears the Cardinal's plot to kill him. In the dark Bosola kills his supposed assassin but finds it is Antonio. Bosola wounds the Cardinal. So does Ferdinand, who then fatally wounds Bosola. Bosola kills Ferdinand, declares revenge complete and dies. Delio declares Antonio's son is rightly his mother's heir.

About the Play

Webster's heroine the Duchess of Malfi is that rare thing in early modern Europe, a woman who exercises independent political power; but this independence is challenged by her two brothers, proud, intemperate and increasingly driven by demons of the unconscious. Webster's play shows humanity expressing its sunniest and its blackest potential in sexual and family relations. The heroine's bid for private domestic happiness provokes jealous reactions from her brothers, increasingly bizarre and cruel, leading to torture, and finally murder, but they cannot break her spirit or divert her from the path of Christian piety. Webster creates deep characters, vivid stage images and magnificent poetry to depict the tragic conflict of darkness and light.

The Tragedy of the Duchess of Malfi was acted by Jacobean London's leading company of actors, Shakespeare's company, the King's Men, probably in 1613, certainly by 1614. The play's setting is a Renaissance Italian court, but with hinted parallels to the scandal-prone Court of King James I at Whitehall. Webster wrote for a theatrically knowledgeable audience – a significant proportion of them women. He used the established conventions of revenge tragedy – the court setting, spying, melancholy, madness, multiple murders – and also created new extreme effects of metaphysical wit, black comedy, and horror, inspired by literary works fashionable with the elite, including Sidney's Arcadia. Webster composes stage action of disturbing symbolic potency, and the fierce clash of passions releases forces of real destructive power.

Critical Introduction

Scepticism

Webster's most important change from his main source, Painter, is a concern with questionable interpretation. Webster poses a general question about metaphysics in his play's many references to saints, witches, devils, omens, ghosts and shrines, which seem to be presented sometimes as superstition, sometimes as having the real efficacy attributed to them by the old religion. The ruined cloister episode (V.iii) and the reference to 'some reverend monument / Whose ruins are even pitied' (IV.ii.33–4) implicitly acknowledge the conflicted cultural-political after-effects of Henry VIII's break with the Catholic Church and

Dissolution of the Monasteries (hauntingly and memorably touched on by Shakespeare in the line from Sonnet 73, 'Bare ruined choirs where late the sweet birds sang').[1]

The Duchess of Malfi gains much from the destabilising energies of scepticism as they engage sharply with a fundamentally religious conception of human life. Webster grants affective force to a whole code of omens and religious signs and images and ceremonies, but his play also absorbs the spirit of the sceptical Montaigne (frequently alluding to his *Essayes*) and it is in touch with Stoicism – written in a cultural moment much concerned with guilt and damnation, with the incorrigible corruption of a darkened world. Some modern scholars interpret the play as showing a Calvinistic bias, whereas others find it not inconsistent with Jacobean Anglicanism.

Webster's play has echoes (noted in the Commentary) of writings by John Donne: *Ignatius*, (1610) – a brief and biting satire against Roman Catholics in general and Jesuits in particular – and *The Anniversaries* (1612), dark religious meditative poems. Donne's family suffered severe persecution for their Catholic faith, and he had recently converted to Anglicanism.[2]

The Duchess of Malfi struck a contemporary spectator, the Italian Orazio Busino, in 1618 as an attack on the Catholic faith and the Church of Rome.[3] A central concern in the play as a whole is with the opposed concepts of fate / accident, substance / emptiness, at a historical moment when Christianity was in doctrinal crisis, when cultural values seemed at hazard, when oblique perspectives were cultivated for their revealing insights. It is, paradoxically, by a process of negation that the Duchess finally achieves the exacting Christian virtue of true contrition: that is, in the words of a great modern Anglican metaphysical poet,

> A condition of complete simplicity
> (Costing not less than everything)[4]

Webster's dramatic fiction is set in Catholic Italy in 1504 (the year specified in the horoscope Antonio draws when his first child is born). At that date in many parts of Italy, a couple could marry, as indeed Webster's

---

1 See Alison Shell, *Catholicism, Controversy and the English Literary Imagination 1558–1660*, 1999; Eamon Duffy, *The Stripping of the Altars*, 1992; also Todd Borlik, ' "Greek is Turned Turk": Catholic Nostalgia in *The Duchess of Malfi* in Luckyj, pp. 136–52.

2 John Carey describes Donne as a man who has renounced a religion, to some manifestations of which he is still, at a profound level, attached. (John Carey, ed., *John Donne, The Major Works*, 1990, pp. xxxv–vi). From a different point of view Marcus, pp. 53–5, compares Webster's Duchess to Donne's poetically idealised Elizabeth Drury.

3 Hunter, pp. 31–2.

4 T. S. Eliot, 'Little Gidding' in *Collected Poems 1909–1962*, 1963, pp. 222–3.

Duchess and Antonio do marry, simply by exchanging rings and vows, followed by consummation – though public acknowledgement was also required. A new ruling for Catholic marriage was made later in the mid-sixteenth century by the Council of Trent, 1563, requiring a Church ceremony conducted in public by a priest.

For Webster's audience in Protestant England the issue of clandestine marriage was topical, for although civil law continued to permit a simple domestic kind of marriage, soon after the accession of King James I in 1604 English canon law on marriage was given tighter definition.[5]

It should be remembered however that the staging of religious ceremonies was forbidden on the Elizabethan stage, so that Webster as playwright was under constraint in what he presented. Still, Webster does go very near staging a marriage – perhaps he took legal advice himself on how close he might go.

The Duchess declares that their marriage is valid in common law *per verba de praesenti* ('by words said in the present'):

> How can the Church build faster?
> We now are man and wife, and 'tis the Church
> That must but echo this.   (I.i. 479–81)

J. W. Lever comments: 'The marriage should have been later solemnised: whether or not this took place we are not told in the play.'[6]

Women and Power

The remarriage of widows was also at this time a matter of contention in England (and is a feature of the plot of *Twelfth Night*). In fact there are numbers of recorded historical instances of English noble widows in this period remarrying, and doing so below their station – one famous and popular case was the Duchess of Suffolk, who in 1552 married her servant.[7]

5 Thereafter, to avoid being clandestine, a marriage required two witnesses, and the threefold publication of banns or the issue of a valid licence, and a ceremony conducted within the diocese in which the couple dwelt and performed in an allowed season and canonical set hours, and only within a lawful church or chapel, and in the presence of a minister of the Church of England. See Martin Ingram, *Church Courts, Sex and Marriage in England, 1570–1640*, 1987, p. 213. Close in date to Webster's play was a sensational case of clandestine marriage: it concerned the nobly born Arbella Stuart (as Lucas notes). She ranked very high in the line of royal succession and therefore needed the king's permission to marry, but King James I refused it. She secretly chose William Seymour and married him in June 1610. The secret got out, the pair were imprisoned, both escaped, but Arbella was quickly re-arrested and imprisoned. She went mad and died in the Tower in 1615.

6 J. W. Lever, *The Tragedy of State*, p. 97.

The Duchess of Malfi begins with a conversation between two courtiers. Webster uses Antonio and Delio here as anchormen and delays the first entrance of the Duchess: when she does appear she and the Cardinal stand on display while Antonio gives a commentary: the Cardinal a villain – as black as his brother Ferdinand – the Duchess their sister the very opposite: the three of them resembling medals. One might wonder whether this emblematic verdict is to be taken straight.

Webster establishes a critical *form of attention*, then gives it an intenser focus by dispensing with the mediation of on-stage observers: it is on an otherwise bare stage Ferdinand hires Bosola, and the brothers menacingly warn the Duchess that 'The marriage night / Is the entrance into some prison' and 'Your darkest actions – nay, your privatest thoughts / Will come to light'. Ferdinand threatens the Duchess with his naked dagger: implying incestuous passion, not just naked patriarchal power.

Now the Duchess (I.i.331–9) alone on that bare stage delivers her soliloquy.[8] Then, a switch to a very unexpected mood – one associated rather with romantic comedy and (ironically enough, here) with its elements of festive anarchy and reversal – she demands Antonio attend the presence, teases him, woos and wins him, thereby excitingly reversing the gender-roles. She also breaks the social and political obligation that the nobility marry their equals: the Duchess installs her servant as her lord and master.[9]

As a widow but one no longer in submissive mourning, the Duchess has full power over her dukedom and her court, power usually held by a man. To invert the normal master–servant relationship is in this particular case the essential precondition for her union, prolonging a tender, companionate, witty relationship, despite its fragile basis in secrecy. But the Duchess is not safe even in her bedchamber. Her pregnancies, the 'natural' fact of her female sexuality, make her vulnerable; and Antonio, once denied status and power, is a shadow of his former self.

Niccolo Machiavelli in his highly influential book *The Prince* (1532), a frankly secular analysis of political power, points out that every prince, in order to survive, must devise plots and practice deception: even in Act I the Duchess is lying when she tells her brothers she will never marry – for

7 Further instances are given in Boklund p.19, Brennan pp. 134–5 and Forker, pp. 299–300. See also Frances E. Dolan in Luckyj p. 125.
8 Since in Q1 Cariola's entry is simply part of a 'massed entry' stage direction, editors of critical editions must choose where exactly to place it. Some editors have her enter with the Duchess at line 282 but I am convinced that it should not be until 339, so that the exchange between the brothers and the Duchess is in private.
9 Later in III.ii.7–8 she jokingly calls him 'a Lord of Misrule' and he replies 'Indeed, my rule is only in the night'. On the ironic significance of the Lord of Misrule, see the note to IV.ii.1.

she must have already conceived the plot to woo and wed Antonio. She may have power, but to keep it, mere wishes cut no ice.

Webster is careful to show that she makes mistakes: is it her humane ideals that fatally distract her? Or her Aragonian pride and self-will that induce her to take the game less seriously than do her opponents? Or does simply being female and marrying mean pregnancies, children? She chooses freely in choosing Antonio. Perhaps excitement about this renders her off-guard in agreeing that Bosola should become her Master of Horse. It seems a small thing – princes, after all, grant favours all the time – but accepting Bosola proves fatal: it was the Cardinal's idea (I.i.215–17) and insinuatingly proposed by Ferdinand.

The Aragon family characteristic is wilfulness. In Ferdinand and the Cardinal it is expressed in deranged violence, yet when the Duchess first shows spirit, has it too an Aragonian tinge? To stress a close physical resemblance between all three, as was done in the RSC productions in 1971 and 1989, seems justifiable from Webster's text: to see in the Duchess a family likeness to, as well as an extreme difference from, her brothers, makes her less the alabaster saint, more human – and conscious of her noble rank. She chooses one man, and hers is a beautiful domesticity. At last alone with Antonio she displays tenderness and a warm sense of humour complicated by wit.

Her proud Aragonian blood gives her the nerve to enter this labyrinth (her own metaphor), but unlike Theseus tracking the Minotaur she lacks prudence, leaves no thread to find her way out again. Hence, between the wooing of Act I and the fragile, happy, married (even grey-haired) flirtatiousness of Act III, Webster interposes so much anxious and nefarious activity: the clouds gather and the prospect darkens.

Act I presents the figure of woman as young, beautiful, noble, articulate and witty, opposed to caricatured male misogyny and arrogance. Act II presents contrastingly harsh images of woman's physicality, in the states of old age, heavy pregnancy, and sexual wantonness: first an Old Lady, a satiric stereotype of ugliness, ageing and disease; then the pregnant Duchess having to make a small joke about her own visibly increasing girth and heavy gait. Bosola has already detected (and been revolted by) physical signs of pregnancy: 'she pukes, her stomach seethes, / The fins of her eyelids look most teeming blue' (II.i.62–3). The diagnosis is confirmed as the audience watch her eating – and eating surprisingly greedily – the apricots that Bosola gives her (apricots had obscene associations in Webster's time). She suddenly feels the onset of labour pains. This is a graphic physical contrast to the poised and happy young woman who courted Antonio. Antonio confides to Delio that the Duchess is suffering 'the worst of torture, pain and fear' (II.ii.62). These events take place at night. Bosola in the darkness hears a woman's screams from the Duchess' lodgings. Her childbirth is presented not as a natural and happy part of love and marriage, but as agonising and very dangerous as well as a threat to her secrecy.

What is emphasised here is a culturally reinforced idea, the natural subjection of women, a symbolic projection of their innocent victimhood as supposedly part of the very scheme of creation. A new female character, Julia, the Cardinal's mistress, serves as a complex and exaggerated parallel to the Duchess.[10] In Julia erotic feeling is simple and forthright lust: her seduction of Bosola at pistol-point (V.ii) suggests an interest in 'rough trade' but it also contains distorted echoes of the Duchess' wooing of Antonio in Act I. Julia (again in parallel with the Duchess) is recklessly prepared in Act V to take the sexual initiative, playing an amoral thrilling trick on the Cardinal, her new lover Bosola a hidden voyeur.

In the Duchess' case erotic desire within marriage harmoniously includes the humane and the maternal (although Webster qualifies this, showing her bold wooing, and the erotic spice added by intimate banter in the presence of Cariola, and the frisson of the game of stealing out of the bedchamber in the dark).

Secrets

Surprise entrances from secret concealment are especially associated with Ferdinand. Immediately after presenting the death of the Duchess Webster shows first its shocking impact on Ferdinand, who enters promptly – because, presumably, he has been secretly watching the whole time; perhaps he is to be imagined lurking constantly behind the door throughout Act IV.

Yet the first to employ spying as a tactic is, ironically, the Duchess herself, in the final episode of Act I. There Cariola brings Antonio to the Duchess and leaves the pair to play their scene apparently alone, though in fact – by the Duchess' direction – Cariola observes and overhears them from concealment; then, just at the point where Antonio and the Duchess agree, Cariola enters again – and this gives Antonio such a shock that he cries out 'Hah'. Cariola also takes part in a subsequent spying episode (though again benevolently intended) in III ii, this time conspiring *with* Antonio *against* the Duchess, when the two of them steal out of the chamber as the Duchess gazes in her mirror.

10 In the 1960 Stratford-on-Avon production Julia was red-wigged like the Duchess to make a visual parallel with her; this also implied, in the Cardinal, unrecognised incestuous tendencies towards his sister, and a close parallel between him and Ferdinand.

Webster likewise bases his plot on secrets – every character has a secret and many episodes in the play present spying or overhearing. In fact the secret status of the marriage itself is a central dynamic of the play's action.

After the death of the Duchess, V.iii presents the extraordinary episode when Antonio and Delio visit a ruined abbey and graveyard. An echo is heard, on the face of it simply an acoustic effect of the ruined walls. To Antonio the echo sounds like the Duchess' voice, and even the audience, like Delio, can recognise that the echoed phrases seem to be a secret warning to Antonio from her ghost. There is ironic allusiveness at a meta-theatrical level also, in this play where so much depends on prefiguring and reflection, on pre-echoes and echoes.[11]

It is the hope for a country far beyond the stars, of which only dim images and echoes are sensed here among the prisons and ruins where fearful mankind live, which animates the Duchess as she confronts her tormentors. As a counterpoint to the incoherence, confusion and horrors in which the play is to end, Antonio in the Echo scene experiences, or dreams, a momentary reunion with his wife: then the vision fades, and night comes again.

Yet to the sceptical Delio the Echo is an acoustic phenomenon, and questionable: indeed it is *more* questionable being only a voice, invisible, than is the ghost which in another tragedy, *Hamlet*, is seen and recognised as well as heard, returning from the 'undiscovered country' of death. The Duchess of Malfi returns (so to speak) not as a forbidding figure clad in armour demanding revenge, but as a feminine voice; and when one searches earlier in the play for a pre-echo of the scene, it turns out to be III.ii, with its haunting 'Never see thee more': this leads to others.[12]

Death

Webster emphasises the different perspectives from which the action can be viewed: the use of Asides, in particular, alerts the audience to the different degrees to which characters understand what is going on, and shows how inevitably misjudgements are made in interpreting what is overheard or seen. This applies even to death, which one might think

11 Beyond being a conceit associating the Duchess with the story of Echo in Ovid, *Metamorphoses*, Echo constitutes a metatheatrical allusion, and a bold one, alluding to Webster's key constructional technique of echoing and repetition, so well analysed by Christina Luckyj, *A Winter's Snake: Dramatic Form in the Tragedies of John Webster*, 1989.

12 The Echo scene is the reverse, as in a mirror, of the episode in III.ii where Antonio (and Cariola) spy helplessly from off-stage as on-stage the Duchess, gazing at her face in her mirror, is threatened by Ferdinand, after which Antonio and Cariola return to comfort her. V.iii reverses this, with the Duchess/Echo off-stage anxious about the on-stage Antonio.

appalling precisely for its stark certainty – as Ferdinand finds it to be on seeing the Duchess dead: 'Cover her face. Mine eyes dazzle. She died young' (IV.ii.250). This is so superbly memorable, so apparently conclusive an utterance. Yet Webster subverts it only a moment later: for after Ferdinand has gone, the Duchess will revive. She was not after all dead, and Ferdinand, for all his obsessively fascinated gaze, was deceived: the Duchess returns to consciousness for a moment, and it is only after Bosola's comforting (if deceiving and false) words that she finally dies breathing the word 'mercy'.

Webster demonstrates that drama is the mode of artistic discourse closest to – indeed mirroring – the real deceptive state of the world as men experience it. The series of disguises and deceptions – the episode in darkness when Ferdinand gives her a severed hand, the traverse drawn to display her husband and children dead, the entry of the Madmen – culminates in the entry of Bosola disguised as an Old Man to make the chilling announcement 'I am come to make thy tomb' and deliver a sermon:

> Thou art a box of worm-seed, at best, but a salvatory of green mummy. What's this flesh? A little cruded milk, fantastical puff-paste . . . Didst thou ever see a lark in a cage? Such is the soul in the body. (IV.ii.115ff.)

Seen as a whole this sequence has a design; it figures the death of the Duchess in terms of an inverted wedding celebration. The Madmen constitute an anti-masque and charivari (see note to IV.ii.1) though these are real madmen, not Jacobean court masque fantastics artificially contrived to entertain King James I – and while they provoke laughter in an audience they are grim victims of spiritual or mental disorder. As Bellman, Bosola gives her macabre presents from her brothers, a coffin, cord and bell. The dirge is the exact inversion of an epithalamion or wedding-song; then follows the pronouncement of the death sentence, strangling; finally, according to this pattern, the noose is a wedding ring of death and the strangling a brutal act of destruction, the exact reverse of the ceremony of marriage itself.

The Duchess, however, exerts her will at the last and intervenes, staging herself consciously in the formal attitude of Christian devotion, kneeling at prayer (like a statue on a family tomb or a religious painting). The addition of the rope round her neck is thereby given a different significance, as an emblem of Christian martyrdom not the instrument of deserved punishment that Ferdinand intends. And the audience may recognise a silent, implicit parallel to the Duchess' wooing of Antonio in 7Act I: there she raised Antonio *from* a kneeling position:

> This goodly roof of yours is too low built,
> I cannot stand upright in't   (I.i.406–7)

Sensing that he was trembling, she urged that there is nothing to fear, *no* suggestion of death:

> This is flesh and blood, sir,
> 'Tis not the figure cut in alabaster
> Kneels at my husband's tomb   (I.i.443–5)

Now in Act IV on the point of death, she treats the noose, the satiric-vengeful wedding ring of death, as a consummation devoutly to be wished. Beside her, the shrouded figure of Bosola, actual executioner-murderer, may double as symbol of Time and Mortality.

The Christian symbolism is clear, though it is something consciously *played*, its poise expresses a supreme feat of will: the fearless resolution shown by the Duchess at death corresponds to many Protestant martyr deaths recorded by Foxe.[13] The impression is at once sharpened by contrast to Cariola when she is dragged in. The audience can contrast Cariola's cowardly betrayal of faith to the very different reaction by the Duchess when earlier shown the bodies of her husband and children – especially since the audience also, at first, must take the dead bodies for real.

Cariola's death is only the first of a succession of contrastingly various deaths by which Webster echoes and mirrors what is evidently the play's key event, the death of the Duchess. This makes the play into a kind of *ars moriendi*,[14] a study of dying considered as an art, a theatrical exploration of the Duchess' meditation

> I know death hath ten thousand several doors
> For men to take their exits   (IV.ii.205–6)

The Cardinal contrives a mocking death for Julia by making her kiss a poisoned Bible, Bosola's sword-thrust in the dark strikes Antonio, the very man he vowed to save – 'Such a mistake as one sees in a play'. The Cardinal's epitaph from Bosola is that he ends 'in a little point, a kind of nothing' and Bosola concludes:

> We are only like dead walls, or vaulted graves,
> That ruined, yields no echo.   (V.v.96–7)

---

13 John Foxe, *Actes and Monuments*, was popularly known as *Foxe's Book of Martyrs*, a work of Protestant history and martyrology first published in English in 1563 and frequently reprinted.

14 See Forker, pp. 339–40; Bettie Anne Doebler, 'Continuity in the Art of Dying: *The Duchess of Malfi*', in *Comparative Drama* 14 (1980) 203–215.

If the Duchess endures suffering, she is not finally broken by it, and if her brothers and Bosola dispense suffering, it is reflected back on to them. It is finally in the brothers and Bosola, not in their intended victim the Duchess, that the torture ends in despair, a sense of inner void, 'a kind of nothing' (V.v.78). Both in direct terms and by ironic parallel and allusion, the figure of the Duchess has multiple significance – a proud ruler, a Christian, a daring lover, a wife and mother, torn by, as she transcends, love of life. She relives her wedding as the noose tightens, in her very subjection she recovers her authority: and she turns her murder into a strangely modern martyrdom.

The Malcontent

A key to the play's exploration of paradox is Bosola, declared at the outset by Antonio to have goodness, although Delio recalls the rumour that he may have committed murder. Bosola himself sounds harsh enough for this in Act I: there his grotesque description of the Aragonian brothers – 'like plum trees that grow crooked over standing pools' – shades into a recognition of himself as just another parasite eager to feed on his hosts – he disgustedly imagines himself hanging on the brothers' ears 'like a horse leech till I were full, and then drop off'. When Ferdinand offers gold Bosola at first resists, or pretends to: the coins are 'devils / Which hell calls angels': but then he caves in and takes the money – 'Thus the devil / Candies all sins o'er' (I.i.266–7).

In Act IV Bosola seems to have a function as Chorus when he reports that the Duchess in her imprisonment is so noble

> As gives a majesty to adversity;
> You may discern the shape of loveliness
> More perfect in her tears than in her smiles;
> She will muse four hours together, and her silence,
> Methinks, expresseth more than if she spake.   (IV.i.6–10)

In Jacobean revenge tragedies generally the figure of the malcontent is not just a hired contract-killer, he is given much more prominence and stronger motivation, interwoven in the drama's whole configuration. What is striking in Webster is that Bosola seems at the beginning a mere assassin; he is only gradually drawn towards the inner world of the heroine; his sense of righteousness and justice is revived by contact with her, but even so he still acts as a tool of villainy and persecution.

Webster seems intent on developing Bosola as a complex, unstable figure undergoing real, violent inner change, though he is unable to reform or destroy the system – in Kafkaesque manner the system devours those who serve it. In the adoption of successive roles Bosola both performs and travesties Christian ritual. In the 1980 Manchester production (Bob Hoskins took the role) he died with a manic laugh.[15]

The Play on the Stage

In Webster's Lifetime

The title-page of the first edition of the play published in 1623 states that it was '*Presented priuatly, at the Black-/Friers; and publiquely, at the Globe*'. The play was performed by the King's Men possibly in 1613 and at the latest by December 1614, because William Ostler, who first acted Antonio, died on 16 December 1614. The second Globe was an open amphitheatre on the south bank of the Thames in Southwark. Its roofed wooden stage projected into the yard and was probably about 43 ft wide by 27 ft deep, backed by a wooden façade which had large doors on each side and probably a central opening; there was also limited playing space at first-floor level and a trapdoor in both stage and roof. From 1609 the King's Men also played at Blackfriars, an indoor playhouse situated within the City itself, and *The Duchess of Malfi* may have been presented there first, in 1613. Performances were usually in the afternoon. Some special Blackfriars performances were given at night, indicating that the stage and the auditorium could and would be well lit artificially by candles.[16] The internal dimensions of the Blackfriars measured 66 ft by 46 ft, including the stage and tiring-house.[17] The Blackfriars stage was much smaller than the Globe's and its audience capacity of barely 600 compared to the Globe's 2,800, so at Blackfriars the atmosphere may have been more intimate, and the style of acting and speaking, and the actor's facial expressions, may have been subtler than in the Globe.[18] At neither house was the *auditorium* darkened for performance; spectators in both houses would have been fully aware of each other.

The Duchess of Malfi has the same conventions for indicating night as do plays at the daylit amphitheatre playhouses – the bringing on of torches, candles or lanterns, augmented by emphasis on darkness in the dialogue. The area towards the rear of the stage in both the Globe and

15 See my previous New Mermaid edition, 2001, p. xlii.
16 I am grateful to Andrew Gurr for discussion on stage conditions at Blackfriars: and see Andrew Gurr, 'The Move Indoors', in Christine Dymkowski and Christie Carson, ed., *Shakespeare in Stages,* 2010, pp. 7–21. On lighting at Blackfriars see also R. B. Graves, *Lighting the Shakespearean Stage 1567–1642,* 1999.
17 See the full account in Andrew Gurr, *Playgoing in Shakespeare's London,* 2004, pp. 31–51.
18 See Tiffany Stern, 'Actors and Audiences on the Stage at Blackfriars' in Paul Menzer, ed., *Inside Shakespeare: Essays on the Blackfriars Stage,* 2006, pp. 35–53.

Blackfriars would have been somewhat less well-lit, especially towards sunset, and this perhaps was where macabre surprises were presented, but for such important episodes the audience would still need to be able to see what happens: in Elizabethan amphitheatre plays generally, night scenes tend indeed to be actually crowded with spectacular business.[19]

This was not a scenic theatre, and the few large stage properties had emblematic rather than realistic significance. Webster requires a chair of state, an altar, a shrine, a tomb, and these would be brought on and off stage as required, and the 'waxwork' bodies would be shown by drawing the traverse curtain, upstage centre. Smaller properties in Webster are also important, constituting almost a visual summary of the story – a wedding-ring and a noose, a blood-spotted handkerchief, a dagger, a severed hand, a jewel, gold coins, a pen, ink and paper, apricots, a horoscope, a casket, mirror, pistol, pall, coffin, poisoned book. Clothes are made significant, as when Delio notes that Antonio is still dressed in the French style, or when the Duchess changes to a non-Italian style of loose-bodied gown to help conceal her pregnancy. Clothes are important when they are taken off, as when the Duchess removes jewels and prepares for bed, or when the Cardinal exchanges his religious robes for a soldier's armour.

An Italian visitor to London, Orazio Busino, describes in 1618 a performance of a play he saw which was evidently *The Duchess of Malfi*; Busino says the players showed the Cardinal 'with a harlot on his knee'; he also says (apparently misunderstanding who Julia is) that the Cardinal was shown giving poison to one of his sisters. Clearly, the robes of a cardinal always make a spectacular visual impact, and it is interesting that Busino sees the play as essentially a hostile presentation of Catholicism: 'all this was acted in condemnation of the grandeur of the church which they despise and in this kingdom hate to the death'. Busino evidently found the stage images impressive and memorable: 'first laying down his cardinal's habit on the altar, with the help of his chaplains, with great ceremoniousness; finally, he has his sword bound on and dons the soldier's sash with so much panache you could not imagine it better done'.[20]

Today

Webster's play continues to be regularly performed by companies large and small, from the National Theatre in 2003 to Eyestrings Theatre in 2012, in productions grand or minimal, orthodox or radical. It was also made as a motion-picture, *Hotel*, by Mike Figgis, (2001), which epitomises one major trend, the Tarantino approach to Webster. In 'The Duchess

19 Lopez, p. 106.
20 Hunter, pp. 31–2.

High and Low'.[21] Roberta Barker uses the broad categories 'high' and 'low' to indicate two general performance trends, characterised by elements of elite culture on the one hand, and popular forms on the other. But today even mainstream productions evidently feel a need to reshape Webster's Act I, as had Prowse's 1985 National Theatre production.

An intelligent, highly imaginative production was directed by Laurie Sansom in 2010 at Northampton (which in turn influenced later productions, as at the Old Vic in 2012 starring Eve Best). This is so vividly described by Eleanor Collins that I wish I had space to quote her review in full.[22] An imaginative feature was Sansom's varied use of madrigal singers as a pervasive presence, a kind of Greek chorus,'waiting on the action, setting scenes and creating atmosphere' – and later gaining real agency: 'creeping and skulking they climb the scaffold around Ferdinand and one of them hands him a dagger', symbolising his encroaching madness and also constituting a malevolent supernatural presence. They also double as the troupe of madmen, then as executioners, reacting to Bosola both attentively and accusingly. Collins notes that this sequence uses the full language of theatre to draw attention to the thin line between the real and the imagined, between 'the credible and the ineffable'.

And now for something completely different: a July evening in a former pharmaceuticals factory in London's Docklands: 'One feels', said a reviewer, 'as if one has reached the rim of the world – a scrubby no man's land of cow parsley and warehouses'. The evening ended with the Duchess of Malfi hanging by her feet in mid-air, 'like a joint in a butcher's shop'[23] – and, I would add, like Tamora's sons in the Deborah Warner production of *Titus Andronicus* (1987) as well as the East End villains hung upside down by gangster Harold Shand (Bob Hoskins) in the movie *The Long Good Friday*. The show, a collaboration between English National Opera and radical theatre company Punchdrunk, was said to be based on Webster's tragedy, with a score by Torsten Rasch. At the factory door each audience member received a white mask and was told it must not be removed. On every floor of the factory, rooms were turned into sets – one was a forest made of 'thickly coiled plastic cables', another a church occupied by instrumental musicians and singers, in semi-darkness. It was deliberately made impossible for audiences to see the action consecutively. For those spectators who succeeded in witnessing it, the finale offered 'swinging incense, scarlet dancers and a hellish host of hanged men'. The production won praise as a 'celebration of

21 Luckyj, pp. 42–65.
22 It appeared in *Cahiers Élizabéthains* 79 (Spring 2011), pp. 86–8.
23 Kate Kellaway, *The Observer*, 18 July 2010.

simultaneity', but at the price of shapelessness. Punchdrunk describe their work as 'immersive'.

Back to the mainstream: the Old Vic in 2012 presented a dark Italian-ate set on several levels, with church music and ceremonial involving swinging thuribles of incense, hooded priests (who recurred throughout) and flickering candles. The Duchess made her first entrance 'bathed in light' – as Billington noted, admiring her star performance in a produc-tion that 'allows Webster's aphoristic poetry to do its vital work'.[24] The severed hand sequence (IV.i.29 ff.) was played in actually complete darkness (as in other recent productions) and sexual encounters were graphic and explicit. The supporting cast, especially Bosola, was weak, and the final act disappointing. Gothic horror was abundant, but affection, wit, laughter – even the Beckettian 'laugh that laughs at the laugh' – less so.

Sources

The story of the Duchess of Malfi is first told in Italian, the twenty-sixth novella in Part One of Bandello's *Novelle* (4 volumes, 1554–73). This was soon adapted in French by François de Belleforest, *Histoires Tragiques*, in 1565. Belleforest's version is four times longer, adds dialogues and soli-loquies, considerably – but with little art – develops the characters of the Duchess and Antonio, adds quantities of sentiment, and expresses moral-istic disapproval of the secrecy of the marriage and that this person of noble blood married a commoner.

Webster's direct source is William Painter's English version, *The second tome of the palace of pleasure*, 1567, following Belleforest. Painter's Duchess disdains the 'light' young gentlemen cavorting on their fine horses in the city of Naples. Though disapproving of her marriage to a commoner, Painter admits she chose 'one of the wisest and most perfect gentlemen that the land of Naples that time brought forth'.

Webster's significant changes to Painter are as follows. His Duchess is emotionally direct in her affectionate and companionable marriage and strong in her Christian faith. Webster gives the brothers exaggerated personalities, and builds up Ferdinand to equal the Cardinal in importance, so that the action now centres on the conflict between, on one side her brothers, on the other the Duchess and Antonio. Webster invents the visit to Malfi in Act I by the Cardinal and Ferdinand, and their hiring of Bosola then, and he combines the wooing and the wedding. He brings forward the discovery of the Duchess' secret (in Painter it is

24 *The Guardian*, 29 March 2012.

delayed until after the birth of her second child). Webster invents the clue, the dropped horoscope (adapting from the dropped handkerchief in Shakespeare's *Othello*) as well as Bosola's detection of it, and introduces a new character, Julia, to reflect aspects of the Duchess and the Cardinal. For the movements leading to the Duchess' arrest Webster follows Painter, but then invents the sequence in which Bosola devises torments for the Duchess, and also the episode when Ferdinand gives her the severed hand. Webster invents Act V's Echo scene, the Julia scene, the accidental manner of Antonio's death, the episode in which the Cardinal is trapped, and the final deaths of the brothers and of Bosola himself (in Painter the brothers live on and Bozola escapes after his efficient contract-killing of Antonio). Finally Webster invents the presentation of Antonio's surviving son as heir to the dukedom of Malfi.

The Author

John Webster was born c. 1578 or 1579. He was the eldest son of a maker of coaches and wagons. The family home and business was in Cow Lane, Smithfield, a noisy, smelly, crowded district of London which included the cattle market and Newgate prison. During this period the coachbuilding trade boomed: Webster's father styled himself 'gentleman' and became a member of the Company of Merchant Taylors. John Webster very probably, therefore, went to the Merchant Taylors' School (though there is no documentary evidence for this). His younger brother Edward earned the honour of becoming a member of the Merchant Taylors by working in the family business, whereas the playwright himself did not join at the normal age but in his late thirties, in 1615, using his father's connections to buy his membership. This was about the time that his father died.

Edward took on the expanding business. It is possible that John may have continued to be involved in the family firm. His membership of the company of Merchant Taylors led to a literary commission, to write the Lord Mayor's pageant in 1624. As late as 1632 a satirist[25] connects Webster to his family roots, holding that Webster's brother refused to lend a coach for a funeral because he 'swore thay all weare hired to conuey / the Malfi Dutches sadly on her way'.

After leaving school Webster probably entered the New Inn and then Middle Temple (one of the Inns of Court) in 1598. Webster's interest in the law continued to be important to him, and this is circumstantial evidence for his having been a student there; but his future was to be in another booming London business – the theatre.

25 Cited in Forker p. 58.

In the records for 1602–3 of Henslowe, the theatre manager/entre-preneur, Webster's name appears as one of the hack playwrights writing in collaboration. In 1604 Webster wrote significant additions to John Marston's play *The Malcontent* (originally written for the boys' company of Blackfriars) when it was acquired by Shakespeare's company, the King's Men, to be acted at the Globe. In the same year Webster collaborated with Dekker on a play, *Westward Ho*, for the fashionable and more expensive boys' company at Paul's, an indoor theatre. This was successful enough to provoke Jonson, Chapman and Marston to write in response *Eastward Ho* (1605) for Blackfriars, and for Dekker and Webster to write a follow-up, *Northward Ho*, for Paul's. Their two plays were published in 1607.

Webster married in 1606, and his first child was born two months after the wedding – a fact which might be interesting in relation to the Duchess' difficulties in keeping her pregnancy secret. The most important period of Webster's work as a playwright begins with the performance of *The White Devil* by Queen Anne's Men at the Red Bull in 1612. Its first reception was disappointing; nevertheless he was working on a new play, *The Duchess of Malfi*, in 1612, when Prince Henry died, and Webster broke off to write the non-dramatic elegy *A Monumental Column* (dedic-ated to the King's current favourite, Robert Carr). Webster may have been influenced, in devising the wax-figures episode (*The Duchess of Malfi* IV.i.54) by the funeral procession in 1612 when a life-size effigy of the deceased Prince Henry, richly clothed, lay on top of his coffin and was borne through the London streets.[26]

The Duchess of Malfi must have been first performed before the end of 1614 because the actor William Ostler, who played Antonio, died on 16 December 1614. The play was an immediate success, and has continued to be so to the present day. In 1615 Webster wrote additions to the sixth edition of Overbury's prose *Characters*. There is speculation that there may be a lost play, *Guise*, in the years before the last of Webster's major works, the play *The Devil's Law Case*, 1617–18.

The Duchess of Malfi and *The Devil's Law Case* were published in 1623. Thereafter Webster continued to write plays, but only in collaboration. He had a success with the striking pageant he undertook for the Merchant Taylors in 1624, *Monuments of Honour*, celebrating the election of their member, John Gore, as Lord Mayor. Exactly where and when Webster died is not known, but it was probably in the 1630s.

26 See David Bergeron, 'The Wax Figures in *The Duchess of Malfi*' SEL 18 (1978), pp. 331–9).

NOTE ON THE TEXT

This edition is based on a fresh analysis of the first quarto of 1623, the only authoritative edition; my copy-text is the British Museum copy of Q1, shelf-mark 644.f.72, collated with the principal subsequent editions. Q1 exists in one uncorrected and two corrected states, designated Q1a, Q1b and Q1c. The second corrected state is found only in sheet G, outer forme. Several substantive press variants are clearly alterations not corrections; the indications are that the author made them and the several other additions which are printed in the margins of Q1. NCW (pp. 451–2) provide an analysis of punctuation patterns to further strengthen Brown's hypothesis that Q1 was set by formes, not *seriatim*, and by two compositors.

In this New Mermaid edition punctuation and spelling are modernised, eliminating capitalised nouns and italicised proper names, regularising speech headings and expanding elisions such as final syllable apostrophes. To provide a performable version of the text – again following New Mermaid Series convention – Q1's group entries ('massed entries') at the head of each scene are replaced by directions at the appropriate places for individual entries. Some added stage directions (indicated by square brackets) are incorporated into the text at appropriate points. The commentary records all substantive changes from Q1. Many verse lines divided between speakers are printed in Q1 as successive short lines; in this edition they are arranged as verse. (The problem is associated with the more supple rhythms of dramatic dalogue in Jacobean drama.) Q1 has a number of prose passages which are set in unjustified lines with a capital letter at the beginning of each. Brown notes (pp. lxv–vi) that there are also verse-lines beginning with lower-case letters at I.i.224 and I.i.226, 'probably due to [the scribe Ralph] Crane's frequent practice of beginning both verse and prose lines with lower-case letters, so that the two kinds of dialogue are not readily distinguished'. Where significant, editorial decisions about text and lineation are recorded in the commentary.

It is a sobering thought for modern editors that Crane intervened in many ways when transcribing dramatic texts, and T. H. Howard-Hill, *Ralph Crane and Some Shakespeare First Folio Comedies*, 1972, concludes that Crane's habits seriously affect the authority of texts printed from his transcripts. The printers' copy for *The Duchess of Malfi* Q1 was virtually certainly a scribal transcript by Ralph Crane – it has group entries for the characters at the head of each scene (but see my note at I.i.80 in the present edition), very few and inadequate stage directions, and heavy punctuation. These features do not correspond to those in Q1 of Webster's *The White Devil*, which almost certainly was set from Webster's manuscript, whereas they do correspond to Crane's practice as a professional scribe elsewhere. Further features in *The Duchess of Malfi* Q1 suggest Crane: the heavy use of parentheses and of a terminal colon especially in short dialogue lines, the unusual use of the hyphen, the use of italic script for headings, songs, letters, titles and proper nouns. The absence of profanities in the play, first noted by G. P. V. Akrigg, contrasts with *The White Devil* which has twenty-four uses of 'God' against *The Duchess of Malfi*'s none, and it is this which makes it almost certain that the play has been censored, most probably because it was to appear in print (see III.v. 79–80 n.). Censoring could have been done by Crane, or by Webster himself, who shows a sustained interest in detail and visited the press on at least one occasion. To reintroduce oaths involving God's name is impossible since one cannot detect all the places where the text has been purged, or know the precise oath used.

ABBREVIATIONS

Boklund	Gunnar Boklund, *'The Duchess of Malfi': Sources, Themes, Characters*, 1962.
Brennan	Elizabeth Brennan, ed., *The Duchess of Malfi*, The New Mermaids, 3rd edition, 1993.
Brown	John Russell Brown, ed., *The Duchess of Malfi*, Revels Plays 1964.
Chapman	Allan Holaday, ed., *The Plays of George Chapman: The Tragedies*, 1987.
Dent	R. W. Dent, *John Webster's Borrowing*, 1960.
Donne, *Ignatius*	John Donne, *Ignatius His Conclave*, 1611.
Donne, *Anniversaries*	In Sir Herbert Grierson, ed. *The Poems of John Donne*, 1933.
E in C	*Essays in Criticism.*
ELH	*English Literary Renaissance.*
ELR	*English Literary History.*
Forker	Charles R. Forker, *Skull Beneath the Skin: The Achievement of John Webster*, 1986.
Gurr	Andrew Gurr, *Playgoing in Shakespeare's London*, 3rd edn, 2004.
Hunter	G. K. and S. K. Hunter, eds., *John Webster, a Critical Anthology*, 1969.
Lopez	Jeremy Lopez, *Theatrical Convention and Audience Response*, 2002.
Lucas	F. L. Lucas, ed., *The Complete Works of John Webster*, 1927.
Luckyj	Christina Luckyj, ed.,'*The Duchess of Malfi*', *A Critical Guide*, 2011.
Marcus	Leah S. Marcus, ed., *The Duchess of Malfi*, 2009.
MLR	*Modern Language Review.*
MP	*Modern Philology.*
Montaigne	Michel de Montaigne, *The essayes or morall, politicke and militarie discourses*, trans. J. Florio, 1600.
NCW	David Carnegie, D. C. Gunby and Antony Hammond, ed., *The Cambridge Edition of the Works of John Webster*, Vol. I, 1995.
N&Q	*Notes and Queries.*
OED	*Oxford English Dictionary.*
Painter	William Painter, *The second tome of the palace of pleasure*, 1567.

PinP	Kathleen McLuskie and Jennifer Uglow, eds., '*The Duchess of Malfi*', *Plays in Performance*, 1989.
Pliny	(Caius Plinius secundus), *The historie of the world*, trans. P. Holland, 1601.
Ren.D	*Renaissance Drama.*
RES	*Review of English Studies.*
RSC	Royal Shakespeare Company.
SEL	*Studies in English Literature.*
SP	*Studies in Philology*
Shakespeare	G. Blakemore Evans, ed., *The Riverside Shakespeare*, 1974.
Sidney	A. Feuillerat, ed., *The Complete Works of Sir Philip Sidney*, 1912–26.
Tilley	M. P. Tilley, *A Dictionary of the Proverbs in England in the Sixteenth and Seventeenth Centuries*, 1950.

The White Devil, The Revenger's Tragedy, The Malcontent, The Changeling, are cited from The New Mermaid editions.

ed.	editorial emendation
Q1	the quarto of 1623 (Q1a uncorrected, Q1b corrected, Q1c second corrected, sheet G outer forme only)
Q2	the quarto of 1640
Q3	the quarto of 1678
Q4	the quarto of 1708
s.p.	speech prefix
s.d.	stage direction

FURTHER READING

Editions

John Russell Brown, ed., *The Duchess of Malfi*, 1964.

Elizabeth Brennan, ed., *The Duchess of Malfi*, 1964, 3rd edn, 1993.

David Carnegie, David Gunby, and Antony Hammond, eds., *The Duchess of Malfi*, 1995.

Brian Gibbons, ed., *The Duchess of Malfi*, 2001.

Frank Kermode, ed., *The Duchess of Malfi*, 2005.

Leah S. Marcus, ed., *The Duchess of Malfi*, 2009.

Staging and Performance

Kathleen McLuskie and Jennifer Uglow, eds., *'The Duchess of Malfi'*, *Plays in Performance*, 1989.

R. B. Graves, *Lighting the Shakespearean Stage 1567–1642*, 1999.

Jeremy Lopez, *Theatrical Convention and Audience Response*, 2002.

Andrew Gurr, *Playgoing in Shakespeare's London*, 3rd ed., 2004.

Hotel, dir. Mike Figgis (2001), DVD, Innovation Film Group, 2005.

John F. Buckingham, *The Dangerous Edge of Things: John Webster's Bosola in Context and Performance*, doctoral thesis, Royal Holloway, Dept of Drama and Theatre, 2011.

Pascale Aebischer and Kathryn Price, eds., *Performing Early Modern Drama Today*, 2012.

Articles and Book-Chapters

Michael Neill, 'Monuments and Ruins as Symbols in *The Duchess of Malfi*' in James Redmond, ed., *Themes in Drama* 4, 1982, pp. 71–87.

Karen Bamford and Alexander Leggatt, ed., *Approaches to Teaching English Renaissance Drama*, 2002.

Reina Green, '"Ears Prejudicate" in *Mariam* and *The Duchess of Malfi*' SEL 43, 2 (2003), 459–74.

Albert H. Tricomi, 'The Severed Hand in Webster's *Duchess of Malfi*' SEL 44 (2004), 347–58.

Garrett A. Sullivan, 'Sleep, Conscience and Fame in *The Duchess of Malfi*' in *Memory and Forgetting in English Renaissance Drama: Shakespeare, Marlowe, Webster*, 2005, pp. 109–131.

Maurizio Calbi, '"That Body of Hers": The Secret, the Specular, the Spectacular in the *Duchess of Malfi* and Anatomical Discourses' in *Approximate Bodies: Gender and Power in Early Modern Drama and Anatomy*, 2005, pp. 1–31.

Susan Zimmerman, 'Invading the Grave' in *The Early Modern Corpse and Shakespeare's Theatre*, 2005, pp. 125–71.

Wendy Wall, 'Just a Spoonful of Sugar: Syrup and Domesticity in Early Modern England', MP 104, 2 (2006), 149–72.

Anja Müller-Wood, ' "All the Ill Man can Invent" John Webster and his Duchess' in *The Theatre of Civilized Excess: New Perspectives on Jacobean Tragedy*, 2007, pp. 59–89.

Laura Tosi, 'Mirrors for Female Rulers: Elizabeth I and the Duchess of Malfi' in Alessandra Petrina, Laura Tosi, and Stephen Orgel, eds., *Representations of Elizabeth I in Early Modern Culture*, 2011, pp. 257–75.

Christina Luckyj, ed., *'The Duchess of Malfi': A Critical Guide*, 2011.

Monographs

J.W. Lever, *The Tragedy of State*, 1971.

Nicholas Brooke, *Horrid Laughter in Jacobean Tragedy*, 1979.

Charles R. Forker, *Skull Beneath the Skin: the Achievement of John Webster*, 1986.

Christina Luckyj, *A Winter's Snake: Dramatic Form in the Tragedies of John Webster*, 1989.

Eamon Duffy, *The Stripping of the Altars*, 1992.

Robert N. Watson, *The Rest is Silence: Death as Annihilation in the English Renaissance*, 1995.

William M. Hamlin, *Tragedy and Scepticism in Shakespeare's England*, 2005.

Thomas Rist, *Revenge Tragedy and the Drama of Commemoration in Reforming England*, 2008.

Adrian Streete, *Protestantism and Drama in Early Modern England*, 2009.

THE
TRAGEDY

OF THE DVTCHESSE
Of Malfy.

As it was Presented priuatly, at the Black-Friers; and publiquely at the Globe, By the Kings Maiesties Seruants.

The perfect and exact Coppy, with diuerse *things Printed, that the length of the Play would* not beare in the Presentment.

VVritten by *John Webster.*

Hora.——*Si quid——*
——*Candidus Imperti si non his vtere mecum.*

LONDON:

Printed by NICHOLAS OKES, for IOHN WATERSON, and are to be sold at the signe of the Crowne, in *Paules* Church-yard, 1623.

Original title-page

priuatly, at the Black-Friers The Blackfriars Theatre, smaller than the Globe, an indoor playhouse ('private' alludes to its select fashionable ambitions) which had been home to a company of boy-actors until it was taken over by the most famous and successful adult acting company, the King's Men, whose base was the Globe Theatre. Probably from 1609 the King's Men acted at Blackfriars in winter (October to March or April when the Court was in London, and the law-courts busy) and at the Globe in summer (when the Court was in the country and the law-courts not in session).

publiquely at the Globe The Globe, a large open amphitheatre-type playhouse on Bankside, erected in 1599 with timbers transferred from the old Theatre in Shoreditch. The Globe burned down on 29 June 1613 (before the supposed date of the first performance of *The Duchess of Malfi*) and a more elaborate second Globe was built on the site; it was in use by June 1614.

perfect and exact Coppy What is really striking is this emphatic claim to present the author's fuller text, restoring the cuts made by the players for performance. It is Webster's dignity as author, not merely playwright, and of his work as literature, not as acting-script, that is given emphasis, and this is further stressed in the epigraph from Horace, in the dedicatory epistle where Webster asserts the enduring worth of his work, and in the commendatory verses from fellow authors who stress the established fame of Webster and his Duchess. The year of publication, 1623, is the same as that for the First Folio of Shakespeare, and may have appealed to Webster for that reason.

Hora . . . mecum Horace, *Epistles*, I vi 67–8: *Si quid novisti rectius istis, candidus imperti; si non, his utere mecum* ('If you know something better than these precepts, be kind and tell me; if not, practice mine with me'). As Lucas suggests, Webster presumably intends to apply this with the sense 'If you know a better play, let's hear it, if not, hear mine'.

DEDICATION

To the right honourable George Harding, Baron Berkeley
of Berkeley Castle and Knight of the Order of the Bath
to the illustrious Prince Charles.

My Noble Lord,

That I may present my excuse why, being a stranger to your   5
Lordship, I offer this poem to your patronage, I plead this warrant:
men who never saw the sea yet desire to behold that regiment of
waters, choose some eminent river to guide them thither, and
make that, as it were, their conduct or postilion; by the like
ingenious means has your fame arrived at my knowledge,   10
receiving it from some of worth who, both in contemplation and
practice, owe to your honour their clearest service. I do not
altogether look up at your title, the ancientest nobility being but a
relic of time past, and the truest honour indeed being for a man to
confer honour on himself: which your learning strives to propagate,   15
and shall make you arrive at the dignity of a great example. I am
confident this work is not unworthy your Honour's perusal: for by
such poems as this, poets have kissed the hands of great princes
and drawn their gentle eyes to look down upon their sheets of
paper, when the poets themselves were bound up in their winding-   20
sheets. The like courtesy from your Lordship shall make you live in
your grave, and laurel spring out of it, when the ignorant scorners
of the Muses, that like worms in libraries seem to live only to
destroy learning, shall wither, neglected and forgotten. This work,
and myself, I humbly present to your approved censure, it being   25
the utmost of my wishes to have your honourable self my weighty
and perspicuous comment; which grace so done me, shall ever be
acknowledged

By your Lordship's in all duty and observance,

John Webster.   30

---

1   *George Harding* (1601–58) became eighth Baron Berkeley in November 1613; the
     significance of Webster's choice of this dedicatee (see Forker, p. 119) was that Harding
     was a direct descendant of the first and second Lords Hunsdon, who had both been
     patrons of the Chamberlain's Men, the acting company honoured in May 1603 by royal
     patronage and thereafter re-named the King's Men (the King's Majesty's Servants).
9   *conduct* conductor.
25   *approved censure* seasoned judgement.

3

COMMENDATORY VERSES

In the just worth of that well deserver Mr John Webster,
and upon this masterpiece of tragedy.

In this thou imitat'st one rich and wise
That sees his good deeds done before he dies.
As he by works, thou by this work of fame
Hast well provided for thy living name.   5
To trust to others' honourings is worth's crime,
Thy monument is raised in thy lifetime,
And 'tis most just: for every worthy man
Is his own marble, and his merit can
Cut him to any figure, and express   10
More art than death's cathedral palaces
Where royal ashes keep their court. Thy note
Be ever plainness, 'tis the richest coat.
Thy epitaph only the title be,
Write 'Duchess': that will fetch a tear for thee,   15
For whoe'er saw this Duchess live and die
That could get off under a bleeding eye?

In Tragaediam.

Ut lux ex tenebris ictu percussa Tonantis,
Illa, ruina malis, claris fit vita poetis.   20

Thomas Middletonus,
Poëta & Chron:
Londiniensis

18–20   *In Tragaediam . . . poetis* To tragedy. As light springs from darkness at the stroke of
the thunderer, / May it (ruin to evil) be life for famous poets.

22–3   *Chron: Londiniensis* Chronologer of London. Thomas Middleton the playwright was
appointed to this post in 1620.

4

To his friend Mr John Webster
Upon his *Duchess of Malfi.*

I never saw thy Duchess till the day
That she was lively bodied in thy play:
Howe'er she answered her low-rated love,   5
Her brothers' anger did so fatal prove;
Yet my opinion is, she might speak more,
But never, in her life, so well before.

Wil. Rowley.

To the reader of the author,   10
and his *Duchess of Malfi.*

Crown him a poet, whom nor Rome nor Greece
Transcend in all theirs, for a masterpiece
In which, whiles words and matter change, and men
Act one another, he, from whose clear pen   15
They all took life, to memory hath lent
A lasting fame to raise his monument.

John Ford.

4   *bodied* embodied.
5-6 *Howe'er ... prove* However eloquently in her real life the Duchess may have defended
     that misalliance which her brothers' anger made so fatal (Lucas).
7   *speak* have spoken.
8   *But ... before* She can never have spoken so well as in your play (Lucas).
9   *Wil. Rowley* A dramatist who collaborated at various times with Webster, Middleton
     and Ford.
14-15 *whiles ... Act* while literature has its fashions and the theatre lasts (Brown).

THE ACTORS' NAMES

Bosola, *J. Lowin.*
Ferdinand, 1 *R. Burbidge.* 2 *J. Taylor.*
Cardinal, 1 *H. Cundaile.* 2 *R. Robinson.*
Antonio, 1 *W. Ostler.* 2 *R. Benfield.*
Delio, *J. Underwood.*
Forobosco, *N. Towley.*
Malateste.
The Marquis of Pescara, *J. Rice.*
Silvio, *T. Pollard.*
The several mad-men, *N. Towley, J. Underwood, etc.*
The Duchess, *R. Sharpe.*
The Cardinal's Mistress, *J. Tomson.*
The Doctor, } *R Pallant.*
Cariola,
Court Officers.
Three young Children.
Two Pilgrims.

The play's first edition strikingly dignifies the actors - it is the first in English to publish a list of the actors' names against their parts. The cast probably comprised fourteen to sixteen men and four boys, assuming some doubling. This list probably dates from a stage revival some time after the death of Burbage on 12 March 1619, perhaps near the date of publication, 1623; it is not part of the original manuscript. Two boys listed were probably too young for the first performance in 1613–14 – Sharpe (born in 1601) was apprenticed to Heminges in 1616, and Pallant, born in 1605, was apprenticed in 1620. When the play was new in 1614 Burbage (Ferdinand) and Lowin (Bosola) were certainly leading members of the company, Burbage having created the roles of Hamlet, Malevole, Othello, Lear, while Lowin, with the company since 1603, had acted Falstaff and Epicure Mammon, and as Bosola must have proved 'a formidable figure' by 1623 (so NCW). Burbage died in 1619 and Taylor took over the role of Ferdinand on joining the company. Cundall (Cardinal) a member of the company since 1598, ceased acting in 1619, after which Richard Robinson succeeded him as Cardinal. The role of the Duchess in 1613–14 may have been created by Robinson, who in 1611 had played a Lady in *The Second Maiden's Tragedy.* Ostler (Antonio) was in his twenties in 1614 and died on 16th December in that year, to be succeeded by Benfield. Underwood was in his twenties in 1613–14, Towley (or Tooley) was active before 1605, Rice was apprenticed to Heminges in 1607, Pollard (Silvio)not before 1613, probably doubled as the Doctor and a Madman. See NCW, 423–7, and Andrew Gurr, *The Shakespeare Company 1594–1642*, 2004, pp. 217–46, also David Kathman, 'How old were Shakespeare's boy actors?', *Shakespeare Survey* 58 (2005), 220–46, and 'Grocers, goldsmiths, and drapers: freemen and apprentices in the Elizabethan theater', *Shakespeare Quarterly* 55 (2004), 220-46.

1. R. Burbidge. 2. J. Taylor. That Burbidge is the first-named indicates he was in the original performance (which took place before Ostler's death on 16 Dec 1614) and the second-named, Taylor, was in a revival some time after the death of Burbidge on 13 March 1619.

Forobosco He has no lines to speak and is only referred to in II.ii.29. Perhaps this is a 'ghost'

[DRAMATIS PERSONAE]

[FERDINAND, *Duke of Calabria, twin brother of the Duchess*
CARDINAL, *their brother*
BOSOLA, *formerly served the Cardinal, now returned from imprisonment in the galleys; then Provisor of Horse to the Duchess, and in the pay of Ferdinand*
ANTONIO, *household steward to the Duchess, then her husband*
DELIO, *his friend, a courtier*
CASTRUCHIO, *an old lord, Julia's husband*
SILVIO, *a courtier*
RODERIGO, *a courtier*
GRISOLAN, *a courtier*
PESCARA, *a marquis*
MALATESTE, *a count*
DOCTOR
DUCHESS OF MALFI, *a young widow, later Antonio's wife, and the twin sister of Ferdinand and sister of the Cardinal*
CARIOLA, *her waiting-woman*
JULIA, *wife of Castruchio and mistress of the Cardinal*
OLD LADY
TWO PILGRIMS
The Duchess' Children – *two boys and a girl*
Eight Madmen: *an astrologer, a lawyer, a priest, a doctor, an English tailor, a gentleman usher, a farmer, a broker*
Officers, Servants, Guards, Executioners, Attendants, Churchmen, Ladies-in-Waiting]

character - Webster altered his original plan in the course of composition and cut the part but forgot to delete the name from this list.

Three young Children The eldest a boy, the middle child a girl, the youngest a babe in arms (see III.v.81: 'sweet armful') presumably represented by a property doll.

CASTRUCHIO The name Castruccio is in Painter who (following Belleforest) thus refers to Petrucci, Cardinal of Siena. Lucas suggests Webster saw it as a suitable name for Julia's old husband because it sounds as if it means 'castrated'. Florio defines the Italian word *castrone* as 'a gelded man . . . a cuckold'.

CARIOLA Florio lists the Italian word *carriolo* or *carriuola* as (among other things) a 'trundle-bed'. In an age when personal servants slept in trundle-beds close to their employers, this name would be apt.

The Duchess' children In III.iii.66 there is reference to a son by her first husband; the boy is called Duke of Malfi. This is possibly a 'ghost character' unless it is he who is referred to at V.v.111–12, although Ferdinand's assertion at IV.ii.270–2 seems incompatible with his existence; see also Delio's remarks, as reported by Pescara, at V.v.105–7.

ACT I, SCENE i

[*Enter* ANTONIO *and* DELIO]

DELIO

You are welcome to your country, dear Antonio;
You have been long in France, and you return
A very formal Frenchman in your habit.
How do you like the French court?

ANTONIO   I admire it:
In seeking to reduce both state and people   5
To a fixed order, their judicious king
Begins at home, quits first his royal palace
Of flatt'ring sycophants, of dissolute
And infamous persons – which he sweetly terms
His Master's masterpiece, the work of heaven –   10
Consid'ring duly that a prince's court
Is like a common fountain, whence should flow
Pure silver drops in general, but if 't chance
Some cursed example poison't near the head,

---

0   s.d. ed. (*Actus Primus. Scena Prima. / Antonio, and Delio, Bosola, Cardinall. Q1*).

0   s.d. Antonio and Delio, like other courtiers, may enter 'as from a tournament' and
be accoutred accordingly: Antonio differently from Delio – see n. 3 below. At the
head of this and all subsequent scenes in Q1 (including the dubious Scene ii – see
note to I.i.79 below) there is a 'massed entry' listing all the persons involved,
irrespective of where they actually make their entrance. This is often a feature of
manuscripts intended for literary use, and is typical of the work of the scribe Ralph
Crane, whose practice it was to use Latin for marking Act and Scene divisions, but
may have been following the author's particular wishes here. Webster's *Devil's Law
Case*, a literary rather than theatrical text and also published in 1623, has Latin
divisions, whereas the first edition of *The White Devil*, 1612, has no divisions.

2   *long in France* The historical Antonio had accompanied Federico, the last Aragonese
king of Naples, into exile in France from 1501 until Federico's death in 1504.

3   *habit* dress: Delio says that Antonio's French clothes set him visibly apart in the
Italian court of Malfi, but is implying that Antonio remains essentially unchanged
by his time abroad. NCW suggest he could be wearing the sign of his office as
steward, a gold chain: the steward's gold chain is only mentioned once, quite late in
the play and then derisively, by an Officer, at III.ii.223, in terms recalling the ridicule
of Malvolio in *Twelfth Night*, II.iii.119–20.

4   ed. (How ... court / I ... it Q1).

5   *state* ruling body, grand council (Brown).

9   *which* Referring to the policy of cleansing the court.

Death and diseases through the whole land spread.   15
And what is't makes this blessed government
But a most provident council, who dare freely
Inform him the corruption of the times?
Though some o'th'court hold it presumption
To instruct princes what they ought to do,   20
It is a noble duty to inform them
What they ought to foresee.

[*Enter* BOSOLA]

                Here comes Bosola,
The only court-gall; yet I observe his railing
Is not for simple love of piety,
Indeed he rails at those things which he wants,   25
Would be as lecherous, covetous, or proud,
Bloody, or envious, as any man,
If he had means to be so.

[*Enter* CARDINAL]

                Here's the Cardinal.

BOSOLA

I do haunt you still.

CARDINAL   So.

BOSOLA   I have done you
Better service than to be slighted thus.   30
Miserable age, where only the reward
Of doing well is the doing of it.

CARDINAL

You enforce your merit too much.

BOSOLA

  I fell into the galleys in your service, where for two years

16–22   from Painter, xiii (Dent).

    23   *court-gall* 'a person who harrasses or distresses the court' (*OED*) – *gall* means bile, but also a sore produced by chafing. As a malcontent Bosola is presumably dressed in black; his appearance indicates his poor reward for service, including the hardship of having been a galley-slave. Antonio and Delio serve as critical commentators on the Duchess' Court; Webster's stagecraft is like Shakespeare's in the opening scene of *Antony and Cleopatra* where Demetrius and Philo, Roman officers in the General's retinue, observe and discuss the feminine Court of the Egyptian Queen Cleopatra and watch her striking entry with their obviously enamoured General, Antony. *railing* abusive language.

31–2   *the reward . . . it* Proverbial – Tilley V81.

together I wore two towels instead of a shirt, with a knot on the   35
shoulder, after the fashion of a Roman mantle. Slighted thus?
I will thrive some way: blackbirds fatten best in hard weather,
why not I, in these dog days?

CARDINAL

Would you could become honest.

BOSOLA

With all your divinity, do but direct me the way to it. I have   40
known many travel far for it, and yet return as arrant knaves as
they went forth, because they carried themselves always along
with them.

[*Exit* CARDINAL]

Are you gone? Some fellows, they say, are possessed with the
devil, but this great fellow were able to possess the greatest devil   45
and make him worse.

ANTONIO

He hath denied thee some suit?

BOSOLA

He and his brother are like plum trees that grow crooked over
standing pools: they are rich, and o'erladen with fruit, but none
but crows, pies and caterpillars feed on them. Could I be one of   50
their flatt'ring panders, I would hang on their ears like a horse-
leech till I were full, and then drop off. I pray leave me. Who
would rely upon these miserable dependences, in expectation
to be advanced tomorrow? What creature ever fed worse than
hoping Tantalus? Nor ever died any man more fearfully than he   55

---

38   *dog days* A period of oppressive and unhealthy hot weather, associated with the dog-star Sirius (Brown).

40–3 *I have . . . them* A contradiction of the proverb that travel broadens the mind: Webster is recalling Montaigne, *Essayes*, p. 119.

41   *arrant* thorough.

45–6 Dent notes a borrowing from Donne, *Ignatius*, 15: Loyola was 'so indued with the Diuell that he was able . . . to possesse the Diuell'.

49   *standing* stagnant.

50   *pies* magpies.

51–2 *horse-leech* blood-sucker.

53   *dependences* The condition of living on promises.

55   *Tantalus* The type of the disappointed man (hence the verb 'tantalise'), punished in Hades by perpetual thirst, though up to his neck in water, and by hunger, though fruit hung just beyond his grasp.
     died (Q1b; did Q1a).

that hoped for a pardon? There are rewards for hawks and dogs
when they have done us service, but for a soldier that hazards
his limbs in a battle, nothing but a kind of geometry is his last
supportation.

DELIO

Geometry? 60

BOSOLA

Ay, to hang in a fair pair of slings, take his latter swing in
the world upon an honourable pair of crutches, from hospital to hospital. Fare ye well sir; and yet do not you scorn
us, for places in the court are but like beds in the hospital,
where this man's head lies at that man's foot, and so lower, 65
and lower. [*Exit*]

DELIO

I knew this fellow seven years in the galleys
For a notorious murder, and 'twas thought
The Cardinal suborned it. He was released
By the French general, Gaston de Foix, 70
When he recovered Naples.

ANTONIO 'Tis great pity
He should be thus neglected, I have heard
He's very valiant. This foul melancholy
Will poison all his goodness, for, I'll tell you,
If too immoderate sleep be truly said 75
To be an inward rust unto the soul,

56 *pardon* (Q1b; pleadon Q1a).
  dogs ed. (dogges, and Q1).
  hawks and dogs In Q1 there is a space at the line-end after *hawkes, and dogges,*
  and whereas the preceding and succeeding lines are printed full out right.
  Presumably Q1's second *and* is an erroneous repetition. Lucas suggests the noun
  horses had dropped out, but type could not have fallen out without movement –
  indeed disintegration – of the whole page of type (as NCW note). The parallel in
  Montaigne, *Essayes*, p. 266, is inconclusive: it is true that the first part does refer to
  men serving better, and for less entreaty, 'then wee vse vnto birdes, vnto horses, and
  vnto dogges' – but then follows the second: 'We share the fruites of our prey with our
  dogges and hawkes, as a meede of their paine and reward of their industry': here
  the word 'horses' is omitted.
64 *like* ed. (likes Q1).
70 *Foix* ed. (*Foux* Q1); Q1's *Foux* is probably a transcription error since the correct
  form of the name appears in Painter. Historically, Gaston de Foix was still a child in
  1501 when Naples was recovered (Brown).
73 *melancholy* A mental disease thought to be due to an excess of black bile (see T.
  Bright, *Treatise of Melancholy*, 1586) but also an affectation – and Ferdinand assumes
  Bosola affects melancholy as a 'garb' at I.i.269.

It then doth follow, want of action
Breeds all black malcontents, and their close rearing,
Like moths in cloth, do hurt for want of wearing.

[*Enter* CASTRUCHIO, SILVIO, RODERIGO *and* GRISOLAN]

DELIO

    The presence 'gins to fill. You promised me   80
    To make me the partaker of the natures
    Of some of your great courtiers.

ANTONIO   The Lord Cardinal's,
    And other strangers', that are now in court,
    I shall.

[*Enter* FERDINAND]

    Here comes the great Calabrian Duke.

FERDINAND

    Who took the ring oft'nest?   85

77–9   Malcontents, having been reared in secret (like moths in cloth) are able to do damage precisely because of the lack of activity (NCW).

79   s.d. ed. (SCENA II. / *Antonio, Delio, Ferdinand, Cardinall, Dutchesse, Castruchio, Silvio, Rodocico, Grisolan, Bosola, Iulia, Cariola.* Q1).

79   s.d. No Exit s.d. is marked in Q1 here. Although lines 78–9 form a sententious couplet, this is not decisive evidence of a scene-end since Q1 has numerous mid-scene couplets which do not mark exits. In Webster's *The White Devil*, too, mid-scene sententious couplets are frequent: Webster evidently liked sententious couplets. The 'massed direction' is significant: as Brown (p. lxv) remarks, no manuscript 'prepared for use in a theatre would have the character-names together at the head of each scene, rather than where they enter individually'. This s.d. is probably just such a massed entry prepared with readers in mind. NCW cogently suggest that the manuscript Ralph Crane was copying had a s.d. for several characters; Crane assumed this implied a scene break, which he marked, following it with one of his habitual massed entry directions. I omit the scene-break, so making Act I an unbroken stage action. It is a possible staging option to have Antonio and Delio exit here and return a moment later in the wake of the minor characters who enter at this point. Marcus opts for the scene break, suggesting it implies 'a subtle shift in time and place'.

80   *presence* the ruler's audience chamber, perhaps indicated by a chair of state upstage.

85   *took the ring* A game introduced by King James I to his court in place of jousting: the galloping horseman had to carry off the suspended ring on the point of his lance. NCW quote Nichols, *The Progresses and Public Processions of Queen Elizabeth*, (1823 repr. New York 1966) II, 549–50: King James' son Prince Charles 'mounted as it were upon a Spanish jennet that takes his swiftnes from the nature of the winde, most couragiously and with much agilitie of hand took the ring clearly four times in five courses'. Webster makes rings important in the play: the Duchess puts a ring on Antonio's finger at the end of Act I, the Cardinal takes one off her finger in III.iv (see lines 35–6), Ferdinand gives the Duchess what she takes to be Antonio's severed hand, with a ring on it, (IV.i.42–4), and the noose (see IV.ii.235) is a ring.

SILVIO

Antonio Bologna, my lord.

FERDINAND

Our sister Duchess' great master of her household? Give him the jewel. When shall we leave this sportive action and fall to action indeed?

CASTRUCHIO

Methinks, my lord, you should not desire to go to war in person.   90

FERDINAND

Now for some gravity. Why, my lord?

CASTRUCHIO

It is fitting a soldier arise to be a prince, but not necessary a prince descend to be a captain.

FERDINAND

No?   95

CASTRUCHIO

No, my lord, he were far better do it by a deputy.

FERDINAND

Why should he not as well sleep, or eat, by a deputy? This might take idle, offensive, and base office from him, whereas the other deprives him of honour.

CASTRUCHIO

Believe my experience: that realm is never long in quiet where   100
the ruler is a soldier.

FERDINAND

Thou told'st me thy wife could not endure fighting.

CASTRUCHIO

True, my lord.

FERDINAND

And of a jest she broke of a captain she met full of wounds – I have forgot it.   105

CASTRUCHIO

She told him, my lord, he was a pitiful fellow to lie like the children of Ismael, all in tents.

---

88   *jewel* The reward for taking the ring; but again Webster may signal irony, as *jewel* could signify virginity and married chastity (as in *Cymbeline*, I.iv.153).

104   s.p. FERDINAND ed. (*Fred* Q1).

107   *children . . . tents* i.e. Arabs (See Genesis 21.9–21), tent-dwellers; with a pun on *tent* meaning a dressing for a wound.

FERDINAND

Why, there's a wit were able to undo all the surgeons of the city:
for although gallants should quarrel, and had drawn their
weapons, and were ready to go to it, yet her persuasions would   110
make them put up.

CASTRUCHIO

That she would, my lord.

[FERDINAND]

How do you like my Spanish jennet?

RODERIGO

He is all fire.

FERDINAND

I am of Pliny's opinion, I think he was begot by the wind, he   115
runs as if he were ballass'd with quicksilver.

SILVIO

True, my lord, he reels from the tilt often.

RODERIGO *and* GRISOLAN

Ha, ha, ha!

FERDINAND

Why do you laugh? Methinks you that are courtiers should be
my touchwood, take fire when I give fire, that is, laugh when I   120
laugh, were the subject never so witty.

CASTRUCHIO

True, my lord, I myself have heard a very good jest and
have scorned to seem to have so silly a wit as to understand it.

111   *put up* sheathe their weapons.
114   s.p. FERDINAND ed. (not in Q1); in Q1 the line is inset as for all lines with a new
        speaker. Presumably the s.p. has been accidentally omitted. It is consistent to give the
        line to Ferdinand in this context where he praises the animal and refers several more
        times to horses and horsemanship. It is unlikely that in Ferdinand's presence
        Castruchio would initiate a topic, and a *Spanish jennet* is a light sporting horse (see
        85 n. above) unsuitable for an old lord like Castruchio.
115   *Pliny's opinion* Pliny writes that Portuguese mares are said to conceive by the west
        wind.
116   It is as if quicksilver (mercury) endows the steed with added speed and liveliness –
        a ship may, like a horse, be said to *run* (as in 'run before the wind') and has ballast
        for stability; *quicksilver* suggests speed, high mobility and value, the opposite to
        cheap heavy material normally used as ballast.
117   *reels from the tilt* Quibbling on *reel* (1) swing about, be unbalanced (2) stagger back;
        and on *tilt* (1) the listing effect of uneven ballast on a ship (2) a blow in jousting (3)
        the act of copulation.
120   *when* only when.

FERDINAND

But I can laugh at your fool, my lord.

CASTRUCHIO

He cannot speak, you know, but he makes faces, my lady cannot   125
abide him.

FERDINAND

No?

CASTRUCHIO

Nor endure to be in merry company, for she says too much
laughing and too much company fills her too full of the
wrinkle.   130

FERDINAND

I would then have a mathematical instrument made for her
face, that she might not laugh out of compass. I shall shortly
visit you at Milan, Lord Silvio.

SILVIO

Your grace shall arrive most welcome.

FERDINAND

You are a good horseman, Antonio; you have excellent riders in   135
France: what do you think of good horsemanship?

ANTONIO

Nobly, my lord; as out of the Grecian horse issued many
famous princes, so, out of brave horsemanship arise the first
sparks of growing resolution that raise the mind to noble
action.   140

FERDINAND

You have bespoke it worthily.

[*Enter* CARDINAL, DUCHESS, CARIOLA, JULIA
and Attendants]

SILVIO

Your brother the Lord Cardinal, and sister Duchess.

CARDINAL

Are the galleys come about?

GRISOLAN

They are, my lord.

FERDINAND

Here's the Lord Silvio is come to take his leave.   145

128–30 prose ed. (Nor . . . saies / Too . . . her / Too . . . wrinckle Q1).
  132 *out of compass* immoderately.
  137 *Grecian horse* the proverbial Trojan horse.

DELIO [*Aside to* ANTONIO]

   Now, sir, your promise: what's that Cardinal?
   I mean his temper? They say he's a brave fellow,
   Will play his five thousand crowns at tennis, dance,
   Court ladies, and one that hath fought single combats.

ANTONIO

   Some such flashes superficially hang on him, for form, but   150
   observe his inward character: he is a melancholy churchman.
   The spring in his face is nothing but the engend'ring of toads.
   Where he is jealous of any man he lays worse plots for them
   than ever was imposed on Hercules, for he strews in his way
   flatterers, panders, intelligencers, atheists, and a thousand such   155
   political monsters. He should have been Pope, but instead of
   coming to it by the primitive decency of the Church, he did
   bestow bribes so largely, and so impudently, as if he would have
   carried it away without heaven's knowledge. Some good he
   hath done.   160

DELIO

   You have given too much of him. What's his brother?

ANTONIO

   The Duke there? A most perverse and turbulent nature;
   What appears in him mirth is merely outside.
   If he laugh heartily, it is to laugh
   All honesty out of fashion.

DELIO   Twins?

ANTONIO   In quality.   165

150   *form* outward appearance. Antonio goes on to offer formal Theophrastian
      Character-sketches of Ferdinand's two siblings (162–202). Brown notes parallels
      from Hall, *Characters*, 1608, showing that Webster followed the Jacobean literary
      vogue for such Character-sketches. Later, in 1615, Webster contributed fresh sketches
      to the sixth (posthumous) edition of Sir Thomas Overbury's *Characters*.

152   *spring . . . toads* i.e. his tears, in others a sign of humanity, are a slime which breeds
      amphibians – assuming *spring* means fountain: Lucas compares Chapman, *Bussy*
      d'Ambois, III.ii.263–5 'that toadpool that stands in thy complexion'. Alternatively or
      additionally, if *spring* means Springtime, then in Ferdinand it generates nothing but
      ugliness and poison. Webster probably remembers *Troilus and Cressida*, II.iii.158–9:
      'I do hate a proud man as I do hate the engend'ring of toads'.

155   *flatterers* ed. (Flatters Q1).
      intelligencers spies.

157   *primitive decency* the pristine early period of morality (Marcus).

165   *In quality* In kind – but they are not twins, though Ferdinand and the Duchess are
      actual twins (see IV.ii.253). Nevertheless Webster probably intended close
      resemblance in appearance and age between the three of them, as visual correlation
      to their psychological and emotional involvement with one another. This physical

He speaks with others' tongues, and hears men's suits
With others' ears: will seem to sleep o'th'bench
Only to entrap offenders in their answers;
Dooms men to death, by information,
Rewards, by hearsay.

DELIO   Then the law to him   170
Is like a foul black cobweb to a spider,
He makes it his dwelling, and a prison
To entangle those shall feed him.

ANTONIO   Most true:
He ne'er pays debts, unless they be shrewd turns,
And those he will confess that he doth owe.   175
Last: for his brother there, the Cardinal,
They that do flatter him most say oracles
Hang at his lips, and verily I believe them,
For the devil speaks in them;
But for their sister, the right noble Duchess,   180
You never fixed your eye on three fair medals
Cast in one figure, of so different temper.
For her discourse, it is so full of rapture
You only will begin then to be sorry
When she doth end her speech, and wish, in wonder,   185
She held it less vainglory to talk much
Than you penance, to hear her. Whilst she speaks,
She throws upon a man so sweet a look,
That it were able raise one to a galliard
That lay in a dead palsy, and to dote   190
On that sweet countenance; but in that look
There speaketh so divine a continence

resemblance was stressed in RSC productions in 1971 and 1989. The contemporary
prejudice against widows remarrying is given extreme expression by Hamlet – see
Hamlet, III iv., for instance 68–9: 'you cannot call it love, / For at your age the heyday
in the blood is tame'.
174   *shrewd* ed. (shewed Q1).
       shrewd turns injuries.
181   *your* ed. (you Q1).
187   *you* ed. (your Q1). The parallel with Guazzo, *The civile conversation of M. Steeven
       Guazzo*, trans. G. Pettie, 1581, (cit. Dent p. 67), indicates that Q1's *your* is an error:
       the Cardinal's devilishness is contrasted to the Duchess' religious virtue. In Guazzo,
       although the Duchess' discourses are said to be 'delightful' and her smile 'sweet'
       enough to attract men, her 'continency' leads men to religious virtue.
       Than you penance Than you hold it spiritually purifying.
189   *galliard* a lively dance.

As cuts off all lascivious and vain hope.
Her days are practised in such noble virtue
That sure her nights, nay more, her very sleeps,   195
Are more in heaven than other ladies' shrifts.
Let all sweet ladies break their flatt'ring glasses
And dress themselves in her.

DELIO   Fie, Antonio,
You play the wire-drawer with her commendations.

ANTONIO
I'll case the picture up, only thus much: 200
All her particular worth grows to this sum,
She stains the time past, lights the time to come.

CARIOLA [*Aside to* ANTONIO]
You must attend my lady in the gallery
Some half an hour hence.

ANTONIO   I shall.

FERDINAND
Sister, I have a suit to you.

DUCHESS   To me, sir?   205

FERDINAND
A gentleman here, Daniel de Bosola,
One that was in the galleys.

DUCHESS   Yes, I know him.

FERDINAND
A worthy fellow h'is. Pray let me entreat for
The provisorship of your horse.

DUCHESS   Your knowledge of him
Commends him, and prefers him.

FERDINAND   Call him hither.   210

                            [*Exit* ATTENDANT]

We are now upon parting. Good Lord Silvio,

---

196   *shrifts* confessions.
197   *glasses* looking-glasses, mirrors.
198   *dress . . . her* (1) use her as a mirror (2) adopt her virtues as their own.
199   *play the wire-drawer* spin out to an excessive degree.
200   *case the picture up* put the picture away in its case.
202   *stains* eclipses, puts into the shade.
204–5   ed. (Some . . . hence / I shall / Sister . . . you / To me Sir Q1).
209   *provisorship of your horse* An important and valuable court appointment: Queen Elizabeth I gave the equivalent post in her court to her favourite, Robert Dudley, later Earl of Leicester.
211   *are* ed. (not in Q1).

Do us commend to all our noble friends
At the leaguer.

SILVIO   Sir, I shall.

[DUCHESS]   You are for Milan?

SILVIO   I am.

DUCHESS

Bring the caroches – we'll bring you down to the haven.

[*Exeunt* ALL *but* FERDINAND *and the* CARDINAL]

CARDINAL

Be sure you entertain that Bosola   215
For your intelligence; I would not be seen in't,
And therefore many times I have slighted him,
When he did court our furtherance – as this morning.

FERDINAND

Antonio, the great master of her household,
Had been far fitter.

CARDINAL   You are deceived in him,   220
His nature is too honest for such business.

[*Enter* BOSOLA]

He comes. I'll leave you.   [*Exit*]

BOSOLA   I was lured to you.

FERDINAND

My brother here, the Cardinal, could never
Abide you.

BOSOLA   Never since he was in my debt.

FERDINAND

May be some oblique character in your face   225
Made him suspect you?

BOSOLA   Doth he study physiognomy?
There's no more credit to be given to th'face
Than to a sick man's urine, which some call

---

213   ed. (At . . . Leagues / Sir . . . shall / You . . . *Millaine* / I am Q1).
       leaguer ed. (leagues Q1) = military camp, especially one engaged in a siege.
213   s.p. DUCHESS ed. (*Ferd* Q1). Attribution of the speech in Q1 to Ferdinand cannot be right since he already knows Silvio's destination (see his preceding speech and line 132–3). If the Duchess speaks this line then her next speech at line 214 is prepared for.
214   *caroches* elegant coaches.
215–6   *entertain . . . intelligence* keep that Bosola on your payroll as your secret agent.
218   *court our furtherance* ask us for reward.
228   *a sick man's urine* Early Modern medical analysis of urine was a proverbial joke – see Shakespeare, *2 Henry IV*, I.ii.1–5.

The physician's whore, because she cozens him.
He did suspect me wrongfully.

FERDINAND   For that   230
You must give great men leave to take their times:
Distrust doth cause us seldom be deceived;
You see, the oft shaking of the cedar tree
Fastens it more at root.

BOSOLA   Yet take heed:
For to suspect a friend unworthily   235
Instructs him the next way to suspect you,
And prompts him to deceive you.

[FERDINAND]   There's gold.

BOSOLA   So:
What follows? Never rained such showers as these
Without thunderbolts i'th'tail of them.
Whose throat must I cut?   240

FERDINAND
Your inclination to shed blood rides post
Before my occasion to use you. I give you that
To live i'th'court here and observe the Duchess,
To note all the particulars of her haviour:
What suitors do solicit her for marriage   245
And whom she best affects. She's a young widow,
I would not have her marry again.

BOSOLA   No, sir?

FERDINAND
Do not you ask the reason, but be satisfied
I say I would not.

BOSOLA   It seems you would create me
One of your familiars.

FERDINAND   Familiar? What's that?   250

229   *cozens* deceives.
236   *next* nearest.
237   s.p. ed. (*Berd* Q1).
238–9 *rained . . . tail* alluding to the shower of gold, in which form Jupiter visited Danae.
230–40 ed. (one line Q1).
241   *rides post* runs ahead.
249–50 ed. (I . . . not / It . . . me / One . . . familiars / Familiar . . . that Q1).
250   *familiars* Quibbling on the senses (1) members of the household (2) familiar spirits
       (3) intimate friends. Presumably Ferdinand's reaction is to (3), he being at this point
       unmoved by the implications of (2): on which see below 302 n.

BOSOLA
    Why, a very quaint invisible devil in flesh:
    An intelligencer.
FERDINAND   Such a kind of thriving thing
    I would wish thee: and ere long thou mayst arrive
    At a higher place by't.
BOSOLA   Take your devils,
    Which hell calls angels: these cursed gifts would make   255
    You a corrupter, me an impudent traitor,
    And should I take these they'd take me to hell.
FERDINAND
    Sir, I'll take nothing from you that I have given.
    There is a place that I procured for you
    This morning, the provisorship o'th'horse.   260
    Have you heard on't?
BOSOLA   No.
FERDINAND   'Tis yours: is't not worth thanks?
BOSOLA
    I would have you curse yourself now, that your bounty,
    Which makes men truly noble, e'er should make
    Me a villain: oh, that to avoid ingratitude
    For the good deed you have done me, I must do   265
    All the ill man can invent. Thus the devil
    Candies all sins o'er: and what heaven terms vile,
    That names he complemental.
FERDINAND   Be yourself:
    Keep your old garb of melancholy, 'twill express
    You envy those that stand above your reach,   270
    Yet strive not to come near 'em. This will gain
    Access to private lodgings, where yourself
    May, like a politic dormouse –

---

251   *quaint* cunning.
255   *angels* The gold coins called nobles, familiarly known as angels, bore the image of St
        Michael killing a dragon. The same pun appears in *The Revenger's Tragedy*, II.i.88:
        'forty angels can make four score devils'.
257   *to* ed. (not in Q1).
261   *on't* ed. (out Q1).
267   *o'er* ed. (are Q1).
268   *complemental* polite accomplishment.
273   *politic* cunning.
        dormouse According to Pliny the dormouse renews its strength and youth by sleeping
        all the winter.

BOSOLA   As I have seen some
Feed in a lord's dish, half asleep, not seeming
To listen to any talk, and yet these rogues   275
Have cut his throat in a dream. What's my place?
The provisorship o'th'horse? Say then my corruption
Grew out of horse dung. I am your creature.

FERDINAND
Away!

BOSOLA
Let good men, for good deeds, covet good fame,   280
Since place and riches oft are bribes of shame.
Sometimes the devil doth preach.   *Exit*

[*Enter* CARDINAL *and* DUCHESS]

CARDINAL
We are to part from you, and your own discretion
Must now be your director.

FERDINAND   You are a widow:
You know already what man is, and therefore   285
Let not youth, high promotion, eloquence –

CARDINAL
No, nor any thing without the addition, honour,
Sway your high blood.

FERDINAND   Marry? They are most luxurious
Will wed twice.

CARDINAL   O fie!

FERDINAND   Their livers are more spotted
Than Laban's sheep.

---

274   *Feed . . . dish* Dine at a lord's table. See *The Malcontent*, II.iii.42–4: 'Lay one into his
        breast shall sleep with him, / Feed in the same dish, run in self faction, / Who may
        discover any shape of danger'.
277   *provisorship* ed. (Prouisors-ship Q1).
282   Proverbial – Tilley D230 and D266.
283–4 *your . . . director* you must rely on your own judgement.
288–90 ed. (Sway . . . blood / Marry . . . luxurious / Will . . . twice / O fie / Their . . . spotted
        / Then . . . sheepe / Diamonds . . . value Q1).
288   *high blood* (1) noble lineage (2) passionate nature.
        luxurious lecherous.
289   *livers* The organ was associated with passions, from lust to love: see *As You Like It*,
        III.ii.422–4.
290   *Laban's sheep* See Genesis 30.31–43; but the phrase probably comes from Whetstone,
        Heptameron (1582): 'a company as spotted as Labans Sheepe' (Dent).

DUCHESS   Diamonds are of most value   290
     They say, that have passed through most jewellers' hands.
FERDINAND
     Whores, by that rule, are precious.
DUCHESS   Will you hear me?
     I'll never marry.
CARDINAL   So most widows say,
     But commonly that motion lasts no longer
     Than the turning of an hourglass: the funeral sermon,   295
     And it, end both together.
FERDINAND   Now hear me:
     You live in a rank pasture here, i'th'court.
     There is a kind of honey-dew that's deadly:
     'Twill poison your fame. Look to't. Be not cunning:
     For they whose faces do belie their hearts   300
     Are witches ere they arrive at twenty years,
     Ay, and give the devil suck.
DUCHESS
     This is terrible good counsel.
FERDINAND
     Hypocrisy is woven of a fine small thread
     Subtler than Vulcan's engine: yet, believe't,   305
     Your darkest actions, nay, your privat'st thoughts,
     Will come to light.
CARDINAL   You may flatter yourself
     And take your own choice: privately be married
     Under the eaves of night.
FERDINAND   Think't the best voyage

292–3   ed. (Whores ... precious / Will ... me / I'll ... marry / So ... say Q1).
293   I assume Q1's colon after *marry* signifies a full-stop, as frequently with Crane: but if the colon is interpreted as indicating interruption the Duchess cannot be convicted of telling a bare-faced lie here.
294   *motion* impulse.
298   *honey-dew* sweet sticky substance found on plants, formerly supposed a kind of dew. In *The Malcontent*, III.ii.27–50, Malevole memorably evokes the luxury of an Italian court: 'The strong'st incitements to immodesty – / To have her bound, incensed with wanton sweets, / Her veins filled high with heating delicates ...'
302   Witches supposedly suckled familiar spirits, usually animals, from an extra nipple.
305   *Vulcan's engine* Vulcan used a net of very fine thread to catch Venus and Mars in adultery.
309   *eaves* ed. (eves Q1) Dent compares Dekker, *The Whore of Babylon*, III.i.158, describing Catholic agents secretly infiltrating England, who 'Flie with the Batt under the eeues of night'.

That e'er you made, like the irregular crab 310
Which, though't goes backward, thinks that it goes right
Because it goes its own way; but observe:
Such weddings may more properly be said
To be executed than celebrated.
CARDINAL   The marriage night
Is the entrance into some prison.
FERDINAND   And those joys, 315
Those lustful pleasures, are like heavy sleeps
Which do forerun man's mischief.
CARDINAL   Fare you well.
Wisdom begins at the end: remember it.   [*Exit*]
DUCHESS
I think this speech between you both was studied,
It came so roundly off.
FERDINAND   You are my sister. 320
This was my father's poniard: do you see?
I'd be loath to see't look rusty, 'cause 'twas his.
I would have you to give o'er these chargeable revels;
A visor and a masque are whispering rooms
That were ne'er built for goodness. Fare ye well – 325
And women like that part which, like the lamprey,
Hath ne'er a bone in't.

314–5   ed. (To ... celibrated / The ... night / Is ... prison / And ... ioyes Q1).
  314   Both these verbs could be used equally of religious rites, but Ferdinand implies the
        alternative meaning of *executed* = put to death.
  318   Alluding to the proverbs 'Think on the end before you begin' (Tilley E125) and
        'Remember the end' (E128).
  319   *studied* prepared in advance, rehearsed. If the brothers take positions on either side
        of the Duchess the episode's general parallels with *The Revenger's Tragedy*, IV.iv.4
        (the interrogation by Vindice and Hippolito, with daggers drawn, of their mother)
        are apparent; at the same time in Webster each brother is driven by a different
        obsession: Ferdinand's is sexual, the Cardinal's is social rank. See also II.v below.
321–2   *poniard ... rusty* If he uses the dagger to kill her, its tempered steel will be bloody
        and start to rust: see Juliet's last words, in *Romeo and Juliet*, V.iii.170. Vindice in *The
        Revenger's Tragedy*, IV.iv.45, sheathing his dagger when his mother begins to weep,
        says 'Brother it rains, 'twill spoil your dagger, house it'.
  323   *chargeable revels* expensive court festivities. The elaborate masques at the court of
        James I were notoriously expensive.
324–5   In *The Revenger's Tragedy*, I.iv.27ff., Antonio describes a court masque 'last revelling
        night' where 'torchlight made an artificial noon' and a murderer wore a mask as
        disguise; and Spurio tells (I.ii.185–6) of a court feast and 'a whispering and
        withdrawing hour / When base male bawds kept sentinel at stairhead'.
  326   *lamprey* an eel-like fish.

DUCHESS	Fie sir!	
FERDINAND	Nay,	

I mean the tongue: variety of courtship.
What cannot a neat knave with a smooth tale
Make a woman believe? Farewell, lusty widow.   [*Exit*]   330

DUCHESS

Shall this move me? If all my royal kindred
Lay in my way unto this marriage
I'd make them my low foot-steps, and even now,
Even in this hate, as men in some great battles,
By apprehending danger have achieved   335
Almost impossible actions – I have heard soldiers say so –
So I, through frights and threat'nings will assay
This dangerous venture. Let old wives report
I winked and chose a husband.

[*Enter* CARIOLA]

                  Cariola,
To thy known secrecy I have given up   340
More than my life, my fame.

CARIOLA   Both shall be safe:

For I'll conceal this secret from the world
As warily as those that trade in poison
Keep poison from their children.

DUCHESS   Thy protestation

Is ingenious and hearty: I believe it.   345
Is Antonio come?

CARIOLA   He attends you.

DUCHESS   Good dear soul.

Leave me: but place thyself behind the arras,

---

329   *tale* Punning on the sense 'penis' (as in e.g. *Romeo and Juliet*, II.iv.97).

333   *foot-steps* steps (up to the altar).

339   *winked* closed my eyes. The proverb 'You may wink and choose' (Tilley W501) meant 'choose blind' – but *wink* also meant 'shut your eyes at wrong', in which case the Duchess anticipates moral condemnation and dismisses it as no better than the prejudice of old wives.

341   *fame* reputation.

341   s.p. CARIOLA ed. (*Carolia* Q1).

345   *ingenious and hearty* sagacious and heartfelt.

347   *arras* curtain – hung across the back of the stage (later, at IV.i.54 s.d. a curtain is drawn to display the figures of Antonio and the children).

Where thou mayst overhear us. Wish me good speed,
For I am going into a wilderness
Where I shall find nor path, nor friendly clew   350
To be my guide.

        [CARIOLA *withdraws behind the arras*]

        [*Enter* ANTONIO]

      I sent for you. Sit down:
Take pen and ink and write. Are you ready?
ANTONIO   Yes.
DUCHESS

  What did I say?
ANTONIO   That I should write somewhat.
DUCHESS

  Oh, I remember:
After these triumphs and this large expense   355
It's fit – like thrifty husbands – we enquire
What's laid up for tomorrow.
ANTONIO

  So please your beauteous excellence.
DUCHESS   Beauteous?

  Indeed I thank you: I look young for your sake.
You have ta'en my cares upon you.
ANTONIO [*Rising*]   I'll fetch your grace   360
The particulars of your revenue and expense.
DUCHESS

  Oh, you are an upright treasurer: but you mistook,
For when I said I meant to make enquiry

---

348 *Where . . . us* The staging recalls two episodes involving Polonius in *Hamlet*, III.i.54ff. and III.iv.6ff.
350 *clew* ball of thread used as a guide (as by Theseus to guide him through the labyrinth).
352–4 ed. (Take . . . ready / Yes / What . . . say / That . . . -what / Oh . . . remember Q1).
355 *these* ed. (this Q1).
     triumphs court festivities.
356 *thrifty husbands* provident managers (of the court and ducal household) – but the Duchess lightly hints at *husband* = marriage partner, the sense in 397.
357 *laid up* in store.
358–69 ed. (So . . . Excellence / Beauteous . . . sake / You . . . you / I'le . . . the / Particulars . . . expence Q1).
359 *for your sake* thanks to you – and with the hinted sense 'for love of you'.
362 *upright* Punning on the fact that Antonio has just stood up (NCW).

What's laid up for tomorrow, I did mean
What's laid up yonder for me.
ANTONIO   Where?
DUCHESS   In heaven.   365
I am making my will, as 'tis fit princes should
In perfect memory, and I pray sir, tell me
Were not one better make it smiling, thus,
Than in deep groans and terrible ghastly looks,
As if the gifts we parted with procured   370
That violent distraction?
ANTONIO   Oh, much better.
DUCHESS
If I had a husband now, this care were quit:
But I intend to make you overseer.
What good deed shall we first remember? Say.
ANTONIO
Begin with that first good deed began i'th'world   375
After man's creation, the sacrament of marriage.
I'd have you first provide for a good husband,
Give him all.
DUCHESS   All?
ANTONIO   Yes, your excellent self.
DUCHESS
In a winding sheet?
ANTONIO   In a couple.
DUCHESS
St Winifred, that were a strange will!   380

364–5   See Matthew 6 particularly 19–21: 'lay up for yourselves treasure in heaven . . . for
        where your treasure is there will your heart be also' – but the whole chapter is highly
        relevant.
370   *procured* were the cause of.
371   *distraction* Q3 (distruction Q1).
372   *quit* Under English law at the time her husband would be owner of all her assets
        (Marcus).
373   *overseer* person appointed under the terms of a will to supervise or assist its
        executors.
378–9   ed. (Give . . . all / All / Yes . . . selfe / In . . . sheete / In . . . cople Q1).
379   *winding sheet* shroud. So making her fit to accompany her dead husband. There was
        apparently a fashion for women to be buried in their wedding sheets – see Clare
        Gittings, *Death, Burial, and the Individual in Early Modern England*, 1984, pp.
        111–12, cit. Michael Neill, *Issues of Death*, 1997, p. 339.
380   *Winifred* ed. (*Winfrid* Q1); Q1 is an error since St Winfred – Wynfrith – was then
        universally known as St Boniface. *St Winifred*, a Welsh saint of the 7th century whose

ANTONIO

    'Twere strange if there were no will in you

    To marry again.

DUCHESS   What do you think of marriage?

ANTONIO

    I take't as those that deny purgatory:

    It locally contains or heaven or hell;

    There's no third place in't.

DUCHESS   How do you affect it?   385

ANTONIO

    My banishment, feeding my melancholy,

    Would often reason thus –

DUCHESS   Pray let's hear it.

ANTONIO

    Say a man never marry, nor have children,

    What takes that from him? Only the bare name

    Of being a father, or the weak delight   390

    To see the little wanton ride a-cock-horse

    Upon a painted stick, or hear him chatter

    Like a taught starling.

DUCHESS   Fie, fie, what's all this?

    One of your eyes is blood-shot, use my ring to't,

                            [*Gives him the ring*]

    They say 'tis very sovereign: 'twas my wedding ring,   395

    And I did vow never to part with it

    But to my second husband.

ANTONIO

    You have parted with it now.

DUCHESS

    Yes, to help your eyesight.

---

head, struck off by Caradoc ap Alauc for refusing his love, was restored to life by St Bruno, and is invoked by the Duchess because she sees an apt parallel with her own situation. Recusant Catholics made defiant pilgrimages to the well of St Winifred. See Andrew Breeze, 'St Winifred of Wales and *The Duchess of Malfi*' N&Q (March 1998) 33–4, and Todd Borlik, 'Catholic Nostalgia in *The Duchess of Malfi*' in Luckyj, 138–9.

383–5   Protestants denied the existence of Purgatory; some proverbs averred that marriage was heaven or hell, others that it was purgatory or hell (Dent).

385   *affect* like, feel about.

386   *banishment* When he accompanied Federico to France (see above 2 n.).

391   *wanton* rogue.

395   *sovereign* efficacious: so gold is believed to cure a stye on an eyelid.

ANTONIO
    You have made me stark blind. 400
DUCHESS
    How?
ANTONIO
    There is a saucy and ambitious devil
    Is dancing in this circle.
DUCHESS   Remove him.
ANTONIO   How?
DUCHESS
    There needs small conjuration when your finger
    May do it: thus –
                  [*She puts her ring upon his finger*]
        – is it fit?
                             He kneels
ANTONIO   What said you?
DUCHESS   Sir, 405
    This goodly roof of yours is too low built,
    I cannot stand upright in't, nor discourse,
    Without I raise it higher. Raise yourself,
    Or if you please, my hand to help you: so.
                           [*He rises*]
ANTONIO
    Ambition, madam, is a great man's madness, 410
    That is not kept in chains and close-pent rooms
    But in fair lightsome lodgings, and is girt
    With the wild noise of prattling visitants
    Which makes it lunatic beyond all cure.
    Conceive not I am so stupid but I aim 415
    Whereto your favours tend: but he's a fool
    That being a-cold would thrust his hands i'th'fire
    To warm them.
DUCHESS   So now the ground's broke
    You may discover what a wealthy mine
    I make you lord of.
ANTONIO   Oh my unworthiness. 420
DUCHESS
    You were ill to sell yourself.
    This dark'ning of your worth is not like that

415   *aim* guess.
420   *of* ed. (off Q1).

Which tradesmen use i'th'city: their false lights
Are to rid bad wares off; and I must tell you,
If you will know where breathes a complete man –   425
I speak it without flattery – turn your eyes
And progress through yourself.

ANTONIO
Were there nor heaven nor hell
I should be honest: I have long served virtue
And ne'er ta'en wages of her.   430

DUCHESS   Now she pays it.
The misery of us that are born great,
We are forced to woo because none dare woo us:
And as a tyrant doubles with his words,
And fearfully equivocates, so we
Are forced to express our violent passions   435
In riddles and in dreams, and leave the path
Of simple virtue which was never made
To seem the thing it is not. Go, go brag
You have left me heartless, mine is in your bosom,
I hope 'twill multiply love there. You do tremble.   440
Make not your heart so dead a piece of flesh
To fear more than to love me. Sir, be confident,
What is't distracts you? This is flesh and blood, sir,
'Tis not the figure cut in alabaster
Kneels at my husband's tomb. Awake, awake, man,   445
I do here put off all vain ceremony
And only do appear to you a young widow
That claims you for her husband; and like a widow,
I use but half a blush in't.

ANTONIO   Truth speak for me,
I will remain the constant sanctuary   450
Of your good name.

DUCHESS   I thank you, gentle love,
And 'cause you shall not come to me in debt,

---

424   *rid . . . off* get rid of bad wares.
443   *flesh and blood* Proverbial: 'To be flesh and blood as others are' (Tilley F367).
444–5 *figure . . . tomb* For this comparison see *Merchant of Venice*, I.i.83–4. It is a further
       unwittingly ironic anticipation of tragedy: the Duchess has referred to her will and
       winding-sheet, Antonio to imprisonment and the visits of madmen; even a cold
       hand will recur – see IV.i.50. Elizabethan sculptures were usually polychrome and
       realistic; on the stage, a stone figure could be represented by an actor, as in *The
       Winter's Tale*, V.iii, and so could a waxwork, as in IV.i.54 below.

Being now my steward, here upon your lips
I sign your *Quietus est.*

[*She kisses him*]

This you should have begged now.   455
I have seen children oft eat sweet-meats thus
As fearful to devour them too soon.

ANTONIO

But for your brothers?

DUCHESS   Do not think of them.

[*Embraces him*]

All discord, without this circumference,
Is only to be pitied and not feared.   460
Yet, should they know it, time will easily
Scatter the tempest.

ANTONIO   These words should be mine,
And all the parts you have spoke, if some part of it
Would not have savoured flattery.

DUCHESS   Kneel.

[CARIOLA *comes from behind the arras*]

ANTONIO   Ha?

DUCHESS

Be not amazed, this woman's of my counsel.   465
I have heard lawyers say a contract in a chamber,
Per verba de presenti, is absolute marriage:
Bless, heaven, this sacred Gordian, which let violence
Never untwine.

---

454   *Quietus est* Latin: 'he is discharged of payment due' – a conventional phrase
      indicating that accounts are correct; but with an ominous undertone: it could also
      refer to release from one's debt to nature, death, as in *Hamlet*, III.i.74.
459   *without this circumference* outside my arms' embrace (also perhaps referring to the
      ring).
463   *parts* particulars.
464   *Kneel* The couple might kneel here, or perhaps at 468, and rise again at 480 (Marcus).
467   *Per ... presenti* A term in canon law, 'by words, as from the present': the Elizabethan
      church recognised as a marriage the simple declaration by a couple that they were
      man and wife, even without a witness. See *Measure for Measure*, I.ii.145ff.: Claudio
      explains how he believes his clandestine marriage to Juliet was 'upon a true contract
      . . .' but a new unjustly severe law brands them criminals. This was a topical issue in
      the year when Shakespeare's play was first performed, 1604, since that was the year
      in which English canon law about marriage was newly tightened up.
      de ed. (not in Q1).
468–9 *Bless ... untwine* The Duchess refers to her hand clasping Antonio's.
468   *Gordian* The oracle decreed that anyone who could loose the knot tied by King
      Gordius would rule Asia. Alexander the Great had to cut it with his sword.

ANTONIO
    And may our sweet affections, like the spheres,   470
    Be still in motion –
DUCHESS   Quickening, and make
    The like soft music –
ANTONIO
    That we may imitate the loving palms,
    Best emblem of a peaceful marriage,
    That ne'er bore fruit divided.   475
DUCHESS
    What can the Church force more?
ANTONIO
    That Fortune may not know an accident
    Either of joy, or sorrow, to divide
    Our fixed wishes.
DUCHESS   How can the Church build faster?
    We now are man and wife, and 'tis the Church   480
    That must but echo this. Maid, stand apart,
    I now am blind.
ANTONIO   What's your conceit in this?
DUCHESS
    I would have you lead your Fortune by the hand
    Unto your marriage bed.
    You speak in me this, for we now are one.   485
    We'll only lie, and talk, together, and plot
    T'appease my humorous kindred; and if you please,
    Like the old tale in Alexander and Lodowick,
    Lay a naked sword between us, keep us chaste.

470–2   The planetary spheres supposedly created music by their perpetual (*still*),
        stimulating (*Quickening*) and unheard (*soft*) harmonious motion.
476   *force* enforce.
479   *build* Q1 (bind Brown) Some editors conjecture that 'bind' stood in Crane's copy but
        that in transcribing he erroneously used too many minim strokes; these the
        compositor interpreted as 'uil': but this is unconvincing – why add a letter 'l' which
        is not a minim? Q1 makes sense (a marriage needs to be firmly built) and should
        stand, even though as some editors argue, 'bind' better relates to the passage's
        concern with tying together.
        faster more strongly and firmly.
487   *humorous* ill-humoured, difficult.
488   i.e. The two friends were so alike they were mistaken for each other. When Lodowick
        married a princess in Alexander's name, he laid a naked (unsheathed) sword each
        night between himself and the princess, because he would not wrong his friend.
        This story of 'The Two Faithful Friends' was made into a ballad, and was the subject
        of a play staged by The Admiral's Men in 1597 (NCW).

Oh, let me shroud my blushes in your bosom,   490
Since 'tis the treasury of all my secrets.

[*Exeunt* DUCHESS *and* ANTONIO]

CARIOLA

Whether the spirit of greatness or of woman
Reign most in her, I know not, but it shows
A fearful madness. I owe her much of pity.   [*Exit*]

490   *shroud* hide from view; but the verb also had the ominous sense 'prepare for burial'
         (OED v.7).
491   s.d. If Cariola remains on stage alone (like the solitary Duchess at 331–9), then added
         emphasis is given to her anxiety that her mistress is showing a *fearful madness*.
         Marcus prefers Q1, where all three remain until 494, as truer to the 'whispering
         room' atmosphere of the play.
494   [*Exit*] ed. (*Exeunt* Q1).

ACT II, SCENE i

[*Enter* BOSOLA *and* CASTRUCHIO]

BOSOLA

You say you would fain be taken for an eminent courtier?

CASTRUCHIO

'Tis the very main of my ambition.

BOSOLA

Let me see: you have a reasonable good face for't already, and
your night-cap expresses your ears sufficient largely. I would
have you learn to twirl the strings of your band with a good   5
grace; and in a set speech, at th'end of every sentence, to hum
three or four times, or blow your nose till it smart again, to
recover your memory. When you come to be a president in
criminal causes, if you smile upon a prisoner, hang him, but if
you frown upon him, and threaten him, let him be sure to   10
'scape the gallows.

CASTRUCHIO

I would be a very merry president.

BOSOLA

Do not sup a-nights, 'twill beget you an admirable wit.

CASTRUCHIO

Rather it would make me have a good stomach to quarrel, for
they say your roaring boys eat meat seldom, and that makes   15
them so valiant. But how shall I know whether the people take
me for an eminent fellow?

---

0   s.d. ed. (ACTUS II. SCENA I. / Bosola, Castruchio, an Old Lady, Antonio, Delio,
     Duchesse, Rodorico, Grisolan. Q1).
1   *courtier* lawyer, judge, identified by the white coif or skull-cap (see line 4 below, *your
     night-cap*) worn by a sergeant-at-law. The usual sense of *courtier* may also apply, as
     senior lawyers might well attend the ruler's court.
2   *main* purpose.
3–11 prose ed. (*Q1 lines ending* already / largely / a / sentence / againe / in / if / scape).
4   *expresses . . . largely* shows off your long ears (and makes you look a complete ass).
5   *twirl . . . band* collar-bands with a string attached were fashionable among courtiers
     and lawyers – Brown cites Jonson, *Cynthia's Revels*, V.iv.158.
14–20 prose ed. (*Q1 lines ending* quarrel / seldome / valiant / me / fellow / it / you / you /
     -caps).
15   *roaring boys* rowdies, yobs, louts.

BOSOLA

I will teach a trick to know it: give out you lie a-dying, and if you hear the common people curse you, be sure you are taken for one of the prime night-caps.   20

[*Enter* OLD LADY]

You come from painting now?

OLD LADY

From what?

BOSOLA

Why, from your scurvy face physic. To behold thee not painted inclines somewhat near a miracle. These in thy face, here, were deep ruts and foul sloughs the last progress. There was a lady in   25 France that, having had the smallpox, flayed the skin off her face to make it more level; and whereas before she looked like a nutmeg grater, after she resembled an abortive hedgehog.

OLD LADY

Do you call this painting?

BOSOLA

No, no, but careening of an old morphewed lady, to make her   30 disembogue again. There's rough cast phrase to your plastic.

OLD LADY

It seems you are well acquainted with my closet?

BOSOLA

One would suspect it for a shop of witchcraft, to find in it the fat of serpents, spawn of snakes, Jews' spittle, and their young children's ordures, and all these for the face: I would sooner eat   35 a dead pigeon, taken from the soles of the feet of one sick of the

---

23–8   prose ed. (*Q1 lines ending* -physicke / neere / rutts / progresse / pockes / leuell / Nutmeg-grater / hedge-hog).
25   *sloughs* muddy holes in the road.
       progress ceremonious royal journey.
30–1   prose ed. (*Q1 lines ending* old / againe / plastique).
30   *but* ed. (but you call Q1; but you call it Q3; but I call it Lucas).
       careening . . . lady giving an old lady's leprous hull a good scraping.
31   *disembogue* put out to sea, on the war-path.
       There's . . . plastic That's coarsely put – rough-cast (lime and gravel) crudely plastered, not your smooth finish.
33–41 prose ed. (*Q1 lines ending* witch-craft / spittle / face / feete / fasting / very / his / his / leafe / -selues).
35   *children's* ed. (children Q1).
36–7   *dead . . . plague* In 1612 when the heir to the English throne Prince Henry lay mortally ill, freshly killed pigeons were applied to the soles of his feet. The same treatment is recommended (for the plague) in *The English Huswife*, 1615.

plague, than kiss one of you fasting. Here are two of you whose
sin of your youth is the very patrimony of the physician, makes
him renew his foot-cloth with the spring, and change his high-
priced courtesan with the fall of the leaf. I do wonder you do   40
not loathe yourselves.
Observe my meditation now.
What thing is in this outward form of man
To be beloved? We account it ominous
If nature do produce a colt, or lamb,   45
A fawn, or goat, in any limb resembling
A man; and fly from't as a prodigy.
Man stands amazed to see his deformity
In any other creature but himself;
But in our own flesh, though we bear diseases   50
Which have their true names only ta'en from beasts –
As the most ulcerous wolf, and swinish measle –
Though we are eaten up of lice, and worms,
And though continually we bear about us
A rotten and dead body, we delight   55
To hide it in rich tissue; all our fear –
Nay all our terror – is, lest our physician
Should put us in the ground, to be made sweet.
[*To* CASTRUCHIO] Your wife's gone to Rome: you two couple
and get you to the wells at Lucca, to recover your aches.   60

[*Exeunt* CASTRUCHIO *and* OLD LADY]

37   *kiss . . . fasting* Fasting supposedly makes bad breath even worse.
39   *foot-cloth* a rich cloth laid over the horse's back and hanging down to the ground,
     protecting the rider from dirt: a mark of high status.
39–40   *high-priced* She is, like the foot-cloth, an expensive status-symbol.
42–58   See *Measure for Measure*, III.i.5ff., where the Duke-as-Friar delivers to young Claudio
     similar advocacy: 'Be absolute for death'. The difference here is that instead of a
     young man there is an old lord and old lady. In performance, if Bosola addresses
     them directly his words will seem calculatedly cruel, but if he stands apart and
     addresses the audience, the two old people will serve as visible instances of man's
     deformity.
52   *ulcerous wolf* The Elizabethan name for a type of ulcer was 'wolf': Webster perhaps
     also makes a covert anticipatory allusion to Ferdinand's lycanthropia.
     measle The disease of measles in humans, also a disease in swine: both diseases
     etymologically confused with *mesel* = leprous (*OED*).
56   *tissue* delicate cloth.
58   *sweet* benign in effect.
59–60   ed. (Your . . . you / To . . . aches Q1).
60   *wells at Lucca* The Italian city was famous as a spa.
     recover your aches The waters are to alleviate the symptoms of venereal disease
     (commonly called 'the bone-ache').

I have other work on foot. I observe our Duchess
Is sick a-days, she pukes, her stomach seethes,
The fins of her eyelids look most teeming blue,
She wanes i'th'cheek, and waxes fat i'th'flank;
And contrary to our Italian fashion   65
Wears a loose-bodied gown. There's somewhat in't.
I have a trick may chance discover it,
A pretty one: I have bought some apricots,
The first our spring yields.

       [*Enter* ANTONIO *and* DELIO *talking apart*]

DELIO   And so long since married?
You amaze me.
ANTONIO   Let me seal your lips for ever,   70
For did I think that anything but th'air
Could carry these words from you, I should wish
You had no breath at all.
   [*To* BOSOLA] Now sir, in your contemplation? You are studying
to become a great wise fellow?   75

BOSOLA

Oh sir, the opinion of wisdom is a foul tetter that runs all over
a man's body: if simplicity direct us to have no evil, it directs us
to a happy being. For the subtlest folly proceeds from the
subtlest wisdom. Let me be simply honest.

ANTONIO

I do understand your inside.   80

BOSOLA

Do you so?

ANTONIO

Because you would not seem to appear to th'world puffed
up with your preferment, you continue this out-of-fashion
melancholy; leave it, leave it.

---

  63   The edges of her eyelids are blue, like those of a pregnant woman (Lucas).
65–6   *contrary . . . gown* Bosola, having listed physical signs associated with pregnancy,
        then observes the Duchess' unusual choice of gown, which could conceal the most
        obvious sign; there is an innuendo in *loose-bodied* = morally loose.
  68   *apricots* ed (apricocks Q1). In Q1's period spelling 'Apricocks' Marcus sees a bawdy
        pun ('cock' = penis) and compares lines 22–6 of Webster's Induction to *The
        Malcontent*.
74–90   prose ed. (*Q1 lines ending* contemplation / fellow / tettor / simplicity / happy / from
        the / honest / in-side / so / world / continue / leave it / any / you / reach / horses /
        suit / me / gallop / tyre).
  76   *tetter* skin eruption.

BOSOLA

Give me leave to be honest in any phrase, in any compliment   85
whatsoever. Shall I confess myself to you? I look no higher than
I can reach: they are the gods that must ride on winged horses,
a lawyer's mule of a slow pace will both suit my disposition and
business, for, mark me, when a man's mind rides faster than his
horse can gallop, they quickly both tire.   90

ANTONIO

You would look up to heaven, but I think
The devil that rules i'th'air stands in your light.

BOSOLA

Oh, sir, you are lord of the ascendant, chief man with the
Duchess, a duke was your cousin-german, removed. Say you
were lineally descended from King Pippin, or he himself, what   95
of this? Search the heads of the greatest rivers in the world, you
shall find them but bubbles of water. Some would think the
souls of princes were brought forth by some more weighty
cause than those of meaner persons; they are deceived, there's
the same hand to them, the like passions sway them; the same   100
reason that makes a vicar go to law for a tithe-pig, and undo his
neighbours, makes them spoil a whole province, and batter
down goodly cities with the cannon.

[*Enter* DUCHESS *with* ATTENDANTS]

DUCHESS

Your arm, Antonio. Do I not grow fat?
I am exceeding short-winded. Bosola,   105
I would have you, sir, provide for me a litter,
Such a one as the Duchess of Florence rode in.

BOSOLA

The Duchess used one when she was great with child.

92   *devil . . . air* So referred to in the Bishop's Bible, Ephesians 2.2: he 'that ruleth in the
      ayre'.
93–103 prose ed. (*Q1 lines ending* ascendant / your / lineally / himselfe / in / water / brought
      / persons / them / makes / tithe-pig / spoile / goodly / Cannon).
93   *lord of the ascendant* the dominant influence, the rising star. In astrology the *lord* is
      the planet of which the associated zodiac sign is at the moment *the ascendant* – is
      entering the 'first house', that part of the sky which is rising above the horizon.
94   *cousin-german, removed* first cousin, once removed.
95   *King Pippin* Died 768: King of the Franks and father of Charlemagne.
97–103 Derived from Montaigne, *Essayes*, p. 274.
103   s.d. The entrance would have added effect if placed at line 97 'Some . . .' (Brown).
104   *fat* An attempt to explain away her advanced state of pregnancy.

DUCHESS
    I think she did – come hither, mend my ruff,
    Here, when? Thou art such a tedious lady –   110
    And thy breath smells of lemon peels – would thou hadst
       done –
    Shall I swoon under thy fingers? I am
    So troubled with the mother.
BOSOLA [*Aside*]   I fear too much.
DUCHESS [*To* ANTONIO]
    I have heard you say that the French courtiers
    Wear their hats on 'fore the King.
ANTONIO   I have seen it.   115
DUCHESS
    In the presence?
ANTONIO
    Yes.
[DUCHESS]
    Why should not we bring up that fashion?
    'Tis ceremony more than duty that consists
    In the removing of a piece of felt.   120
    Be you the example to the rest o'th'court,
    Put on your hat first.
ANTONIO   You must pardon me:
    I have seen, in colder countries than in France,
    Nobles stand bare to th'prince; and the distinction
    Methought showed reverently.   125
BOSOLA
    I have a present for your grace.
DUCHESS   For me sir?
BOSOLA
    Apricots, madam.
DUCHESS   Oh sir, where are they?
    I have heard of none to-year.
BOSOLA [*Aside*]   Good, her colour rises.

111   *peels* ed. (pils Q1; peel Q4).
113   *the mother* hysteria.
      too ed. (to Q1).
114   *courtiers* ed. (courties Q1).
118   s.p. ed. (not in Q1, but added by hand in many copies).
125   *Methought* ed. (My thought Q1).
126–8 ed. (I . . . Grace / For me sir / Apricocks Madam / O . . . they / I . . . yeare / Good . . .
       rises Q1).

DUCHESS

Indeed I thank you, they are wondrous fair ones.
What an unskilful fellow is our gardener,   130
We shall have none this month.

BOSOLA

Will not your grace pare them?

DUCHESS

No – they taste of musk, methinks, indeed they do.

BOSOLA

I know not: yet I wish your grace had pared 'em.

DUCHESS

Why?   135

BOSOLA

I forgot to tell you, the knave gardener,
Only to raise his profit by them the sooner,
Did ripen them in horse dung.

DUCHESS   Oh you jest.

You shall judge: pray taste one.

ANTONIO   Indeed madam,

I do not love the fruit.

DUCHESS   Sir, you are loath   140

To rob us of our dainties: 'tis a delicate fruit,
They say they are restorative?

BOSOLA

'Tis a pretty art, this grafting.

DUCHESS

'Tis so: a bett'ring of nature.

BOSOLA

To make a pippin grow upon a crab,   145
A damson on a blackthorn.
[*Aside*]   – How greedily she eats them!
A whirlwind strike off these bawd farthingales!

138–40   ed. (Did . . . –doung / Oh . . . iest / You . . . one / Indeed Madam / I . . . fruit / Sir . . .
         loath).
   141   *dainties* (1) choice foods (2) luxuries – with a sexual innuendo.
   143   *grafting* Ironically alluding to the union of the Duchess with someone of inferior
         stock (see *The Winter's Tale*, IV.iv.86ff.); this verb also had an indecent sense, played
         upon here.
145–6   An instance of Webster's detailed use of sources, here Breton, *Wil of Wit*, 1606, Iir:
         'Is not the Damson tree . . . aboue the Blackthorne tree? is not the Pippin . . . aboue
         the crabtree? the Abricock above the common plum?' (cited by Dent).
   147   *farthingales* hooped petticoats.

For, but for that, and the loose-bodied gown,
I should have discovered apparently
The young springal cutting a caper in her belly.   150

DUCHESS

I thank you, Bosola, they were right good ones,
If they do not make me sick.

ANTONIO   How now madam?

DUCHESS

This green fruit and my stomach are not friends.
How they swell me!

BOSOLA [*Aside*]   Nay, you are too much swelled already.

DUCHESS

Oh, I am in an extreme cold sweat.

BOSOLA   I am very sorry.   155

DUCHESS

Lights to my chamber. Oh, good Antonio,
I fear I am undone.   *Exit*

DELIO   Lights there, lights.
                    [*Exeunt all but* ANTONIO *and* DELIO]

ANTONIO

O my most trusty Delio, we are lost.
I fear she's fall'n in labour, and there's left
No time for her remove.

DELIO   Have you prepared   160
Those ladies to attend her, and procured
That politic safe conveyance for the midwife
Your Duchess plotted?

ANTONIO   I have.

DELIO

Make use then of this forced occasion.
Give out that Bosola hath poisoned her   165
With these apricots: that will give some colour
For her keeping close.

ANTONIO   Fie, fie, the physicians
Will then flock to her.

DELIO   For that you may pretend
She'll use some prepared antidote of her own,
Lest the physicians should re-poison her.   170

149   *apparently* clearly.
150   *springal* stripling.

42

ANTONIO

I am lost in amazement. I know not what to think on't.

Exeunt

[ACT II,] SCENE ii

[*Enter* BOSOLA]

BOSOLA

So, so: there's no question but her tetchiness, and most vulturous eating of the apricots, are apparent signs of breeding.

[*Enter* OLD LADY]

Now?

OLD LADY

I am in haste, sir.

BOSOLA

There was a young waiting-woman had a monstrous desire to 5
see the glass-house –

OLD LADY

Nay, pray let me go –

BOSOLA

And it was only to know what strange instrument it was should swell up a glass to the fashion of a woman's belly.

OLD LADY

I will hear no more of the glass-house, you are still abusing 10
women.

BOSOLA

Who I? No, only by the way, now and then, mention your frailties. The orange tree bears ripe and green fruit and blossoms altogether, and some of you give entertainment for

---

0   s.d. ed. (*SCENA. II. / Bosola, old Lady, Antonio, Rodorigo, Grisolan: seruants, Delio, Cariola.* Q1).
1–3   prose ed. (*Q1 lines ending* teatchiues / apparant / now).
4   This Old Lady is in haste to act as midwife to the Duchess: entering by one door, she is crossing the stage to exit at another when Bosola blocks her way.
6   *glass-house* glass factory: Webster alludes to the Blackfriars glass factory in *The White Devil*, I.ii.132.
13   *bears* ed. (beare Q1).
14   *altogether* both together, simultanously.
    entertainment sexual pleasure.

43

pure love; but more, for more precious reward. The lusty spring   15
smells well, but drooping autumn tastes well. If we have the
same golden showers that rained in the time of Jupiter the
Thunderer, you have the same Danaes still, to hold up their laps
to receive them. Didst thou never study the mathematics?

OLD LADY

What's that, sir?   20

BOSOLA

Why, to know the trick how to make a many lines meet in one
centre. Go, go; give your foster-daughters good council: tell
them that the devil takes delight to hang at a woman's girdle
like a false rusty watch, that she cannot discern how the time
passes.   25

[*Exit* OLD LADY]

[*Enter* ANTONIO, DELIO, RODERIGO, GRISOLAN]

ANTONIO

Shut up the court gates.

RODERIGO   Why sir, what's the danger?

ANTONIO

Shut up the posterns presently, and call
All the officers o'th'court.

GRISOLAN   I shall, instantly.   [*Exit*]

ANTONIO

Who keeps the key o'th'park gate?

RODERIGO   Forobosco.

ANTONIO

Let him bring't presently.   30

[*Exeunt* ANTONIO *and* RODERIGO]

[*Enter* SERVANTS]

SERVANT

Oh gentlemen o'th'court, the foulest treason!

---

15   *precious reward* gold.
17–19   Receiving Jupiter in the form of a shower of gold, Danae became a synonym for a
          mercenary woman. See I.i.238.
18   *Danaes* ed. (Danes Q1).
21–2   *many . . . centre* Proverbial; as in Montaigne, *Essayes*, p. 514: 'a Centre whereto all
          lines come'.
27   *presently* at once.

BOSOLA

If that these apricots should be poisoned, now, without my knowledge!

SERVANT

There was taken even now a Switzer in the Duchess' bedchamber. 35

2 SERVANT

A Switzer?

SERVANT

With a pistol in his great codpiece!

BOSOLA

Ha, ha, ha.

SERVANT

The codpiece was the case for't.

2 SERVANT

There was a cunning traitor: who would have searched his 40 codpiece?

SERVANT

True, if he had kept out of the ladies' chambers; and all the moulds of his buttons were leaden bullets.

2 SERVANT

Oh wicked cannibal: a fire-lock in's codpiece?

SERVANT

'Twas a French plot, upon my life! 45

2 SERVANT

To see what the devil can do!

[*Enter* ANTONIO, RODERIGO, GRISOLAN]

ANTONIO

All the officers here?

SERVANTS   We are.

ANTONIO   Gentlemen,

We have lost much plate, you know; and but this evening

37   *pistol . . . codpiece* The Elizabethan pronunciation of *pistol* omitted the medial 't' –
      so Kökeritz, *Shakespeare's Pronunciation*, 1953, p. 135 – making the pun on *pizzle* =
      penis clearer. The *codpiece*, no longer fashionable by 1612, was sometimes
      exaggerated in size and ornamentation – Rabelais has a memorable passage on
      Gargantua's opulent codpiece. Perhaps the joke involves not only the exaggerated
      size of the codpiece but also the unduly modest endowment of the Switzer in this
      department.

44   *cannibal* Marcus suggests a pun on 'cannonball'.

45   *French* Presumably alluding to the 'French disease', syphilis.

47   *All* Q1 (Are all Q4); *officer*s Q2 (offices Q1).

Jewels to the value of four thousand ducats
Are missing in the Duchess' cabinet. 50
Are the gates shut?
SERVANT   Yes.
ANTONIO   'Tis the Duchess' pleasure
Each officer be locked into his chamber
Till the sun-rising, and to send the keys
Of all their chests, and of their outward doors,
Into her bedchamber: she is very sick. 55
RODERIGO
At her pleasure.
ANTONIO
She entreats you take't not ill. The innocent
Shall be the more approved by it.
BOSOLA
Gentleman o'th'wood-yard, where's your Switzer now?
SERVANT
By this hand, 'twas credibly reported by one o'th'Black-guard. 60
                    [*Exeunt all but* DELIO *and* ANTONIO]
DELIO
How fares it with the Duchess?
ANTONIO   She's exposed
Unto the worst of torture, pain, and fear.
DELIO
Speak to her all happy comfort.
ANTONIO
How I do play the fool with mine own danger!
You are this night, dear friend, to post to Rome, 65
My life lies in your service.
DELIO   Do not doubt me.
ANTONIO
Oh, 'tis far from me: and yet fear presents me
Somewhat that looks like danger.
DELIO   Believe it,
'Tis but the shadow of your fear, no more:
How superstitiously we mind our evils: 70

---

50   *cabinet* private chamber.
59   *Gentleman o'th' wood-yard* Bosola is clearly mocking the Servant's first words (lines
      31 and 34–5 above), so presumably the *wood-yard* has base and menial associations,
      like the next line's joke on *Black-guard* = scullions and greasy turnspits.
68   *looks* Q2 (looke Q1).

The throwing down salt, or crossing of a hare,
Bleeding at nose, the stumbling of a horse
Or singing of a cricket, are of power
To daunt whole man in us. Sir, fare you well:
I wish you all the joys of a blessed father   75
And, for my faith, lay this unto your breast:
Old friends, like old swords, still are trusted best.   [*Exit*]

[*Enter* CARIOLA]

CARIOLA
Sir, you are the happy father of a son.
Your wife commends him to you.
ANTONIO   Blessed comfort:
For heaven' sake tend her well. I'll presently   80
Go set a figure for's nativity.

                                              Exeunt

[ACT II,] SCENE iii

[*Enter* BOSOLA *with a dark lantern*]
BOSOLA
Sure I did hear a woman shriek: list, ha?
And the sound came, if I received it right,
From the Duchess' lodgings. There's some stratagem
In the confining all our courtiers
To their several wards. I must have part of it,   5
My intelligence will freeze else. List again:
It may be 'twas the melancholy bird,

74   *whole man* resolution.
77   s.d. Q4 adds *with a Child*, but this is superfluous: Cariola's appearance is momentary and the dramatic function is not to display the child but to prompt Antonio to make the horoscope, since this is the focus of the next piece of plot.
81   *set . . . nativity* cast his horoscope.

0   s.d. ed. (SCENA. III. / Bosola, Antonio. Q1; Bosola, Antonio, with a dark lanthorn Q4).
0   s.d. *dark lantern* A lantern with an arrangement for concealing its light. On the Elizabethan stage the conventional signal that a scene takes place by night was for actors to carry a light. A dark lantern features again in V.iv.50ff., offering an ironic comment on Bosola's nocturnal and murky career in the play.

Best friend of silence, and of solitariness,
The owl, that screamed so –

[*Enter* ANTONIO, *with a horoscope*]

Ha? Antonio?

ANTONIO
I heard some noise: who's there? What art thou? Speak.   10
BOSOLA
Antonio? Put not your face nor body
To such a forced expression of fear;
I am Bosola, your friend.
ANTONIO   Bosola?
[*Aside*] This mole does undermine me – heard you not
A noise even now?
BOSOLA   From whence?
ANTONIO   From the Duchess' lodging.   15
BOSOLA
Not I. Did you?
ANTONIO   I did, or else I dreamed.
BOSOLA
Let's walk towards it.
ANTONIO   No. It may be 'twas
But the rising of the wind.
BOSOLA   Very likely.
Methinks 'tis very cold, and yet you sweat.
You look wildly.
ANTONIO   I have been setting a figure   20
For the Duchess' jewels.
BOSOLA   Ah: and how falls your question?
Do you find it radical?
ANTONIO   What's that to you?
'Tis rather to be questioned what design,

---

  9   s.d. ed. (Enter *Antonio*, with a Candle his sword drawn Q4).
15–18 ed. (A . . . now / From whence / From . . . lodging / Not . . . you / I . . . dream'd / Let's
       . . . it / No . . . 'twas / But . . . winde / Very likely Q1).
 17   *it* The door by which Antonio entered, and which leads to the Duchess' apartments.
20–2   ed. (You . . . wildly / I . . . figure / For . . .Iewells / Ah . . question / Doe . . radicall /
       What's . . you Q1).
20–1   *setting . . . jewels* Recourse to astrology supposedly enabled the discovery of lost
       goods. Antonio backs up this lie by referring to his earlier – false – claim (see
       II.ii.48ff.) that jewels had been stolen.
 22   *radical* fit to be judged.

When all men were commanded to their lodgings,
Makes you a night-walker.

BOSOLA   In sooth I'll tell you: 25
Now all the court's asleep, I thought the devil
Had least to do here. I came to say my prayers,
And if it do offend you I do so,
You are a fine courtier.

ANTONIO [*Aside*]   This fellow will undo me. –
You gave the Duchess apricots today,   30
Pray heaven they were not poisoned.

BOSOLA   Poisoned?
A Spanish fig for the imputation.

ANTONIO
Traitors are ever confident till they
Are discovered. There were jewels stolen too.
In my conceit none are to be suspected   35
More than yourself.

BOSOLA   You are a false steward.

ANTONIO
Saucy slave, I'll pull thee up by the roots!

BOSOLA
May be the ruin will crush you to pieces.

ANTONIO
You are an impudent snake indeed, sir!
Are you scarce warm and do you show your sting?   40

[BOSOLA
    ...]

ANTONIO
You libel well, sir.

---

25 *night-walker* nocturnal rogue or criminal.
31–4 ed. (Pray . . poysond / Poysond . . . figge / For . . . imputation / Traitors . . . confident
     / Till . . . too Q1).
 · 32 *Spanish fig* An indecent gesture, thrusting the thumb between the first two fingers –
     and with a pun on the other meaning, poison (as in *The White Devil*, IV.ii.60).
41 s.p. BOSOLA ed. (not in Q1) In Q1 two consecutive speeches are given to Antonio,
     probably implying that a speech by Bosola is missing, one provoking Antonio's angry
     response 'You libel well, sir' (Lucas). Brown speculates that 39–40 might have
     belonged to Bosola, referring to Antonio the upstart, but Compositor A, who has
     trouble with s.p.s elsewhere, might have misplaced a s.p. Marcus (presumably
     developing this idea of Brown's) does assign line 40 'Are . . . sting' to Bosola, assuming
     a missing s.p. rather than a missing speech.
42–4 ed. (You . . . sir / No sir / Copy . . . to't / My . . . count Q1).

49

BOSOLA   No, sir. Copy it out
    And I will set my hand to't.
ANTONIO [*Aside*]   My nose bleeds.
                    [*Takes out handkerchief and drops paper*]
    One that were superstitious would count
    This ominous, when it merely comes by chance: 45
    Two letters that are wrought here for my name
    Are drowned in blood:
    Mere accident. [*Aloud*] For you, sir, I'll take order:
    I'th'morn you shall be safe. [*Aside*] 'Tis that must colour
    Her lying in: [*Aloud*] sir, this door you pass not.   50
    I do not hold it fit that you come near
    The Duchess' lodgings till you have quit yourself.
    'The great are like the base, nay, they are the same,
    When they seek shameful ways to avoid shame'.   *Exit*
BOSOLA
    Antonio here about did drop a paper: 55
    Some of your help, false friend:
                    [*Searches with the lantern and finds paper*]
                        – oh, here it is.
    What's here? A child's nativity calculated?
    [*Reads*] *The Duchess was delivered of a son, 'tween the hours twelve
        and one, in the night, Anno Dom: 1504,* (that's this year)
        decimo nono Decembris, (that's this night) *taken according to*   60
        the meridian of Malfi (that's our Duchess: happy discovery).

42–3   *Copy . . . to't* If Antonio will write down the supposed libel Bosola will sign it.
   43   s.d. Developed from the implications in the text: the two letters are *wrought* (46), that
        is, embroidered, *here*, in the handkerchief with which Antonio stanches his nose
        bleed. Antonio drops *a paper* – identified by Bosola as the horoscope in line 57 – and
        it is simple and plausible that he does so when getting out his handkerchief).
        Webster's use of the handkerchief is no doubt intended to recall *Othello* – both the
        likeness and difference are significant.
47–8   ed. (Are . . . order Q1).
   50   *this door* The one to the Duchess' lodging, referred to in line 17 above.
   56   *false friend* The dark lantern.
58–65   As it turns out, this first-born child survives at the end of the play – but for how
        much longer? The prediction for a short life and a violent death remains; *Caetera non
        scrutantur* ('the rest is not examined') means only that the horoscope has not been
        completed, not that its validity is uncertain. Webster's main interest is in what the
        astrological terminology can contribute to the general atmosphere of menace; the
        horoscope is implausible, astrologically speaking: NCW refer to J. C. Eade, *The
        Forgotten Sky*, 1984, pp. 188–9.

> *The Lord of the first house, being combust in the ascendant,*
> *signifies short life; and Mars being in a human sign, joined to*
> *the tail of the Dragon, in the eighth house, doth threaten a*
> *violent death. Caetera non scrutantur.* 65

Why now 'tis most apparent. This precise fellow
Is the Duchess' bawd. I have it to my wish.
This is a parcel of intelligency
Our courtiers were cased up for. It needs must follow
That I must be committed on pretence 70
Of poisoning her, which I'll endure, and laugh at.
If one could find the father now: but that
Time will discover. Old Castruchio
I'th'morning posts to Rome; by him I'll send
A letter that shall make her brothers' galls 75
O'erflow their livers. This was a thrifty way.
'Though lust do masque in ne'er so strange disguise
She's oft found witty, but is never wise'. *[Exit]*

[ACT II,] SCENE iv

[*Enter* CARDINAL *and* JULIA]

CARDINAL
Sit: thou art my best of wishes. Prithee tell me
What trick didst thou invent to come to Rome

---

62   *Lord . . . house* See II.i.93 n. This planet was supposed to be particularly influential
     in the life of the child then born.
     combust burnt up. This signifies a planet positioned within 8 degrees of the sun,
     whereby its influence is destroyed.
63   *human sign* Aquarius, Gemini, Virgo or Sagittarius.
64   *tail of the Dragon* This lay where the moon traverses the ecliptic in its descent. It had
     a sinister influence.
     eighth ed. (eight Q1).
     eighth house This regularly signified death.
66   *precise* strict, puritanical.
69   *cased* ed. (caside Q1).

0   s.d. ed. (SCENA. IIII. / Cardinall, and Iulia, Seruant, and Delio. Q1).
1   *Sit* Orazio Busino (7 Feb 1618) reports seeing a performance where the Cardinal,
     presumably at this point, was shown 'with a harlot on his knee'. Recent productions
     have developed such possibilities further: in the Manchester Royal Exchange

Without thy husband.

JULIA   Why, my lord, I told him
I came to visit an old anchorite
Here, for devotion.

CARDINAL   Thou art a witty false one –   5
I mean, to him.

JULIA   You have prevailed with me
Beyond my strongest thoughts; I would not now
Find you inconstant.

CARDINAL   Do not put thyself
To such a voluntary torture, which proceeds
Out of your own guilt.

JULIA   How, my lord?   10

CARDINAL
You fear my constancy because you have approved
Those giddy and wild turnings in yourself.

JULIA
Did you e'er find them?

CARDINAL   Sooth, generally, for women,
A man might strive to make glass malleable
Ere he should make them fixed.

JULIA   So, my lord.   15

CARDINAL
We had need go borrow that fantastic glass
Invented by Galileo the Florentine
To view another spacious world i'th'moon,
And look to find a constant woman there.

JULIA
This is very well, my lord.

CARDINAL   Why do you weep?   20
Are tears your justification? The self-same tears
Will fall into your husband's bosom, lady,
With a loud protestation that you love him
Above the world. Come, I'll love you wisely,
That's jealously, since I am very certain   25

production 1980 the couple mimed sexual coition before speaking, in the RSC
production of 1989/90 Julia advanced on the Cardinal, raising her skirts by degrees
before sitting astride a chair to display her legs to him.
12   *turnings* ed. (turning Q1).
16   *fantastic glass* The telescope built by Galileo in 1609.
18   Dent compares Donne, *Ignatius*, 116–7: 'hills woods, and Cities in the new world, the
     Moone'.

You cannot me make cuckold.
JULIA   I'll go home
To my husband.
CARDINAL   You may thank me, lady:
I have taken you off your melancholy perch,
Bore you upon my fist, and showed you game,
And let you fly at it. I pray thee kiss me.   30
When thou wast with thy husband thou wast watched
Like a tame elephant – still you are to thank me –
Thou hadst only kisses from him, and high feeding,
But what delight was that? 'Twas just like one
That hath a little fingering on the lute,   35
Yet cannot tune it – still you are to thank me.
JULIA
You told me of a piteous wound i'th'heart
And a sick liver, when you wooed me first,
And spake like one in physic.
                                    [*Knocking*]
CARDINAL   Who's that?
Rest firm: for my affection to thee,   40
Lightning moves slow to't.

[*Enter* SERVANT]

SERVANT   Madam, a gentleman
That's come post from Malfi, desires to see you.
CARDINAL
Let him enter, I'll withdraw.   *Exit*
SERVANT   He says
Your husband Old Castruchio is come to Rome,
Most pitifully tired with riding post.   [*Exit*]   45

[*Enter* DELIO]

JULIA

28–30 *perch . . . at it* As if she were a falcon.
   30   *thee* ed. (the Q1).
  31–2 *watched . . . elephant* The comparison of Julia to an elephant is grotesque, with *tame* implying 'sexually frustrated'; *watched* could mean 'tamed by being kept awake' and also 'looked at' (like the real elephant put on public exhibition in London in 1594, which attracted great attention).
   38   *liver* The seat of love and the passions.

Signior Delio? [*Aside*] 'Tis one of my old suitors.

DELIO

    I was bold to come and see you.

JULIA   Sir, you are welcome.

DELIO

    Do you lie here?

JULIA   Sure, your own experience

    Will satisfy you no, our Roman prelates

    Do not keep lodging for ladies.

DELIO   Very well: 50

    I have brought you no commendations from your husband,

    For I know none by him.

JULIA   I hear he's come to Rome?

DELIO

    I never knew man and beast, of a horse and a knight,

    So weary of each other; if he had had a good back

    He would have undertook to have borne his horse,   55

    His breech was so pitifully sore.

JULIA   Your laughter

    Is my pity.

DELIO   Lady, I know not whether

    You want money, but I have brought you some.

JULIA

    From my husband?

DELIO   No, from mine own allowance.

JULIA

    I must hear the condition ere I be bound to take it.   60

DELIO

    Look on't, 'tis gold, hath it not a fine colour?

JULIA

    I have a bird more beautiful.

DELIO

    Try the sound on't.

JULIA   A lute-string far exceeds it,

    It hath no smell, like cassia or civet,

    Nor is it physical, though some fond doctors   65

47–8   ed. (I . . . you / Sir . . . wel-come / Do . . . here / Sure . . . experience Q1).

  47   *you* ed. (your Q1).

  65   *physical* used as medicine.

Persuade us seeth't in cullisses; I'll tell you,
This is a creature bred by –

[*Enter* SERVANT]

SERVANT   Your husband's come,
  Hath delivered a letter to the Duke of Calabria that,
  To my thinking, hath put him out of his wits.   [*Exit*]
JULIA
  Sir, you hear: 70
  Pray let me know your business, and your suit,
  As briefly as can be.
DELIO   With good speed. I would wish you,
  At such time as you are non-resident
  With your husband, my mistress.
JULIA
  Sir, I'll go ask my husband if I shall,   75
  And straight return your answer.   *Exit*
DELIO   Very fine.
  Is this her wit, or honesty, that speaks thus?
  I heard one say the Duke was highly moved
  With a letter sent from Malfi. I do fear
  Antonio is betrayed. How fearfully   80
  Shows his ambition now: unfortunate Fortune!
  'They pass through whirlpools, and deep woes do shun,
  Who the event weigh, ere the action's done'.   *Exit*

66   *seeth't* ed. (seeth's Q1).
       cullisses broths.
77–80 This soliloquy seems to suggest that Delio is on a mission of espionage, and possibly
       plans to manipulate Julia (indeed in V.ii Bosola succeeds in doing this); but no more
       emerges of the present intrigue. This may be deliberate on Webster's part, and
       designed to create an atmosphere of secret plotting.
82   *pass through* successfully cross.

[ACT II,] SCENE v

[*Enter*] CARDINAL, *and* FERDINAND *with a letter*

FERDINAND
I have this night digged up a mandrake.
CARDINAL   Say you?
FERDINAND
And I am grown mad with't.
CARDINAL   What's the prodigy?
FERDINAND
Read there: a sister damned, she's loose i'th'hilts,
Grown a notorious strumpet!
CARDINAL   Speak lower.
FERDINAND   Lower?
Rogues do not whisper't now, but seek to publish't,   5
As servants do the bounty of their lords,
Aloud; and with a covetous searching eye
To mark who note them. Oh confusion seize her!
She hath had most cunning bawds to serve her turn,
And more secure conveyances for lust   10
Than towns of garrison, for service.
CARDINAL   Is't possible?
Can this be certain?
FERDINAND   Rhubarb, oh, for rhubarb
To purge this choler! Here's the cursed day
To prompt my memory, and here it shall stick
Till of her bleeding heart I make a sponge   15
To wipe it out.

---

0   s.d. ed. (SCENA V. / Cardinall, and Ferdinand, with a letter. Q1).
1   *digged* Q1b (dig Q1a).
     mandrake The forked root of the plant mandragora, supposedly resembling a man,
     gave rise to the superstition that when dug up it emitted a shriek which induced
     madness.
2   *prodigy* ed. (progedy Q1).
3   *loose i'the hilts* unchaste.
4   ed. (Growne . . . Strumpet / Speak lower / Lower Q1).
11   *service* supplies (including sexual services).
12   *rhubarb* A recognised antidote to choler.

CARDINAL   Why do you make yourself
  So wild a tempest?
FERDINAND   Would I could be one,
  That I might toss her palace 'bout her ears,
  Root up her goodly forests, blast her meads,
  And lay her general territory as waste   20
  As she hath done her honours.
CARDINAL   Shall our blood,
  The royal blood of Aragon and Castile,
  Be thus attainted?
FERDINAND   Apply desperate physic!
  We must not now use balsamum, but fire,
  The smarting cupping glass, for that's the mean   25
  To purge infected blood, such blood as hers.
  There is a kind of pity in mine eye,
  I'll give it to my handkercher –
              [*He wipes away the tears with a handkerchief*]
                       and now 'tis here,
  I'll bequeath this to her bastard.
CARDINAL   What to do?
FERDINAND
  Why, to make soft lint for his mother's wounds,   30
  When I have hewed her to pieces.
CARDINAL   Cursed creature!
  Unequal nature, to place women's hearts
  So far upon the left side.
FERDINAND   Foolish men,
  That e'er will trust their honour in a bark
  Made of so slight weak bullrush as is woman,   35
  Apt every minute to sink it!
CARDINAL   Thus
  Ignorance, when it hath purchased honour,
  It cannot wield it.

---

23   *attainted* The Cardinal intends the legal term referring to lineage stained or
     corrupted; Ferdinand takes it literally, referring to blood infected with disease (with
     the added sense of *blood* = passion).
28   s.d. Webster stresses the action, ironically recalling Antonio's fatal use of his
     handkerchief for the nosebleed in II.iii.
30   *mother's* ed. (mother Q1).
33   *left* Probably to be understood figuratively, as sinister, not right (see III.i.28–9).
36–7 ed. (Apt . . . it / Thus / Ignorance . . . honour Q1).

FERDINAND   Methinks I see her laughing –
  Excellent hyena! Talk to me somewhat quickly,
  Or my imagination will carry me   40
  To see her in the shameful act of sin.
CARDINAL   With whom?
FERDINAND
  Happily with some strong-thighed bargeman;
  Or one o'th'woodyard that can quoit the sledge
  Or toss the bar; or else some lovely squire
  That carries coals up to her privy lodgings.   45
CARDINAL
  You fly beyond your reason.
FERDINAND   Go to, mistress,
  Tis not your whore's milk that shall quench my wild-fire,
  But your whore's blood!
CARDINAL
  How idly shows this rage, which carries you
  As men conveyed by witches through the air   50
  On violent whirlwinds! This intemperate noise
  Fitly resembles deaf men's shrill discourse,
  Who talk aloud, thinking all other men
  To have their imperfection.
FERDINAND   Have not you
  My palsy?
CARDINAL Yes. I can be angry   55
  Without this rupture; there is not in nature
  A thing that makes man so deformed, so beastly,
  As doth intemperate anger. Chide yourself.
  You have diverse men who never yet expressed
  Their strong desire of rest, but by unrest –   60
  By vexing of themselves. Come, put yourself
  In tune.
FERDINAND So, I will only study to seem

43 *o'th'* ed. (the Q1).
    quoit the sledge throw the hammer.
45 *carries coals* With a subsidiary (proverbial) sense 'do any dirty or menial work' – see
    next note.
    privy lodgings private apartment (with puns on *privy* parts = genitals, and *lodgings*
    = sexual penetrations).
48–50 ed. (But ... blood / How ... rage / Which ... ayre Q1).
55 *palsy* the shaking palsy, involuntary tremors (*OED* sb 1a).
56 *rupture* Q1 (rapture conj. Dyce).

The thing I am not. I could kill her now
In you, or in myself, for I do think
It is some sin in us heaven doth revenge   65
By her.
CARDINAL Are you stark mad?
FERDINAND   I would have their bodies
Burnt in a coal pit with the ventage stopped,
That their cursed smoke might not ascend to heaven;
Or dip the sheets they lie in, in pitch or sulphur,
Wrap them in't and then light them like a match;   70
Or else to boil their bastard to a cullis
And give't his lecherous father to renew
The sin of his back.
CARDINAL   I'll leave you.
FERDINAND   Nay, I have done.
I am confident, had I been damned in hell
And should have heard of this, it would have put me   75
Into a cold sweat. In, in, I'll go sleep.
Till I know who leaps my sister, I'll not stir:
That known, I'll find scorpions to string my whips,
And fix her in a general eclipse.

                                                    Exeunt

ACT III, SCENE i

[*Enter* ANTONIO *and* DELIO]

ANTONIO

    Our noble friend, my most beloved Delio,
    Oh you have been a stranger long at court;
    Came you along with the Lord Ferdinand?

DELIO

    I did sir; and how fares your noble Duchess?

ANTONIO

    Right fortunately well. She's an excellent   5
    Feeder of pedigrees: since you last saw her,
    She hath had two children more, a son, and daughter.

DELIO

    Methinks 'twas yesterday – let me but wink
    And not behold your face, which to mine eye
    Is somewhat leaner, verily I should dream   10
    It were within this half hour.

ANTONIO

    You have not been in law, friend Delio,
    Nor in prison, nor a suitor at the court,
    Nor begged the reversion of some great man's place,
    Nor troubled with an old wife, which doth make   15
    Your time so insensibly hasten.

DELIO   Pray sir tell me,
    Hath not this news arrived yet to the ear
    Of the Lord Cardinal?

ANTONIO   I fear it hath.
    The Lord Ferdinand that's newly come to court
    Doth bear himself right dangerously.

---

   0   s.d. ed. (ACTVS III. SCENA I. / Antonio, and Delio, Duchesse, Ferdinand, Bosola.
        Q1).
   2   Delio has been away in Rome since the end of II.ii.
6–11   Comic-ironic in-jokes on the conventions of theatrical illusion, by which some two
        years must be imagined to have passed since II.ii – in performance time, it certainly
        is 'within the half-hour' that Antonio and Delio last met! (See Lopez, pp. 75–6).
 17ff. This discussion is clearly parallel to that between Delio and Antonio about good
        government in Act I, but here Antonio seems to be admitting that keeping the
        marriage secret has seriously weakened the Duchess as ruler, even without the new
        danger of Ferdinand's presence.

DELIO	Pray why?	20

ANTONIO

He is so quiet that he seems to sleep
The tempest out as dormice do in winter.
Those houses that are haunted are most still
Till the devil be up.

DELIO   What say the common people?

ANTONIO

The common rabble do directly say   25
She is a strumpet.

DELIO   And your graver heads,
Which would be politic, what censure they?

ANTONIO

They do observe I grow to infinite purchase
The left-hand way, and all suppose the Duchess
Would amend it if she could. For, say they,   30
Great princes, though they grudge their officers
Should have such large and unconfined means
To get wealth under them, will not complain
Lest thereby they should make them odious
Unto the people; for other obligation –   35
Of love, or marriage, between her and me –
They never dream of.

[*Enter* DUCHESS, FERDINAND *and* BOSOLA]

DELIO   The Lord Ferdinand
Is going to bed.

FERDINAND   I'll instantly to bed,
For I am weary. I am to bespeak
A husband for you.

DUCHESS   For me, sir? Pray who is't?   40

FERDINAND

The great Count Malateste.

DUCHESS   Fie upon him!
A Count? He's a mere stick of sugar candy,

---

27   *be* ed. (he Q1).
28   *purchase* wealth.
29   *left-hand* corrupt.
31–5 Dent compares the close parallel in Donne, *Ignatius,* 92.
37   *of* ed. (off Q1).
39   *bespeak* ed. (be be-speake Q1).

You may look quite thorough him. When I choose
A husband, I will marry for your honour.

FERDINAND

You shall do well in't. – How is't, worthy Antonio?   45

DUCHESS

But, sir, I am to have private conference with you
About a scandalous report is spread
Touching mine honour.

FERDINAND   Let me be ever deaf to't:
One of Pasquil's paper bullets, court calumny,
A pestilent air which princes' palaces   50
Are seldom purged of. Yet, say that it were true:
I pour it in your bosom, my fixed love
Would strongly excuse, extenuate, nay deny
Faults, were they apparent in you. Go be safe
In your own innocency.

DUCHESS   Oh bless'd comfort,   55
This deadly air is purged.

                    Exeunt [all but FERDINAND *and* BOSOLA]

FERDINAND   Her guilt treads on
Hot burning coulters. Now Bosola,
How thrives our intelligence?

BOSOLA   Sir, uncertainly:
'Tis rumoured she hath had three bastards, but
By whom, we may go read i'th'stars.

FERDINAND   Why some   60
Hold opinion all things are written there.

BOSOLA

Yes, if we could find spectacles to read them.
I do suspect there hath been some sorcery
Used on the Duchess.

FERDINAND   Sorcery? To what purpose?

---

49   *Pasquil's paper bullets* satires or lampoons (*Pasquin* or *Pasquil* became a popular
      name for a satirist, following the custom in 16th century Rome of attaching
      lampoons to a statue named after one Pasquino or Pasquillo, a sharp-tongued
      schoolmaster or cobbler).

54   *were* ed. (where Q1).

56–7 *reads . . . coulters* An ordeal decreed as a trial of chastity in Old English law; the
      mother of Edward the Confessor is reputed to have walked barefoot upon nine
      coulters red hot. The coulter is the cutting blade in front of a ploughshare.

57   *coulters* ed. (cultures Q1).

BOSOLA

    To make her dote on some desertless fellow   65
    She shames to acknowledge.

FERDINAND   Can your faith give way
    To think there's power in potions or in charms
    To make us love, whether we will or no?

BOSOLA

    Most certainly.

FERDINAND

    Away! These are mere gulleries, horrid things   70
    Invented by some cheating mountebanks
    To abuse us. Do you think that herbs or charms
    Can force the will? Some trials have been made
    In this foolish practice, but the ingredients
    Were lenitive poisons, such as are of force   75
    To make the patient mad; and straight the witch
    Swears, by equivocation, they are in love.
    The witchcraft lies in her rank blood. This night
    I will force confession from her. You told me
    You had got, within these two days, a false key   80
    Into her bedchamber?

BOSOLA   I have.

FERDINAND   As I would wish.

BOSOLA

    What do you intend to do?

FERDINAND   Can you guess?

BOSOLA   No.

FERDINAND

    Do not ask then.
    He that can compass me, and know my drifts,
    May say he hath put a girdle 'bout the world   85

---

75   *lenitive poisons* drugs seemingly aphrodisiac but inducing madness. N. W. Bawcutt
    in MLR 66, (1971) 488–91, claims that Webster is recalling Shelton's translation of
    Don Quixote, I.iii.8: 'poysons . . . cause men runne mad, and in the meane while
    perswade us they have force to make one love well'. Lucas notes that Webster in
    Anything for a Quiet Life, I.i.91, uses *lenitive* to mean 'soothing', but finds this goes
    oddly with *poisons*: is Webster guilty of false etymology, via Latin *lenare* = to
    prostitute? The phrase could then mean 'violent aphrodisiac'.

And sounded all her quicksands.

BOSOLA   I do not
Think so.

FERDINAND
What do you think then, pray?

BOSOLA   That you are
Your own chronicle too much, and grossly
Flatter yourself.

FERDINAND   Give me thy hand, I thank thee.   90
I never gave pension but to flatterers
Till I entertained thee: farewell.
'That friend a great man's ruin strongly checks,
Who rails into his belief, all his defects'.

Exeunt

[ACT III,] SCENE ii

[*Enter* DUCHESS, ANTONIO *and* CARIOLA]

DUCHESS
Bring me the casket hither, and the glass.
You get no lodging here tonight my lord.

ANTONIO
Indeed I must persuade one.

DUCHESS   Very good.
I hope in time 'twill grow into a custom
That noblemen shall come with cap and knee   5
To purchase a night's lodging of their wives.

ANTONIO
I must lie here.

86–90   ed. (And . . . -sands / I . . . not / Thinke so / What . . . pray / That . . . are / Your . . .
        grosly / Flatter . . . selfe / Give . . . thee Q1).

Act III scene ii
   0   s.d. ed. (*SCENA. II. / Dutchesse, Antonio, Cariola, Ferdinand, Bosola, Officers. Q1*).
   0   s.d. The Duchess will remove her jewellery and brush her hair in preparation for
        bed; candles or torches would indicate that it is night.

DUCHESS   Must? You are a Lord of Misrule.
ANTONIO
  Indeed, my rule is only in the night.
DUCHESS
  To what use will you put me?
ANTONIO   We'll sleep together.
DUCHESS
  Alas, what pleasure can two lovers find in sleep?   10
CARIOLA
  My lord, I lie with her often and I know
  She'll much disquiet you –
ANTONIO   See, you are complained of –
CARIOLA
  For she's the sprawling'st bedfellow.
ANTONIO
  I shall like her the better for that.
CARIOLA
  Sir, shall I ask you a question?
ANTONIO   I pray thee Cariola.   15
CARIOLA
  Wherefore still when you lie with my lady
  Do you rise so early?
ANTONIO   Labouring men
  Count the clock oft'nest, Cariola,
  Are glad when their task's ended.
DUCHESS   I'll stop your mouth.
                                    [*Kisses him*]

ANTONIO
  Nay, that's but one, Venus had two soft doves   20
  To draw her chariot: I must have another.
                                    [*She kisses him*]
  When wilt thou marry, Cariola?
CARIOLA   Never, my lord.
ANTONIO
  Oh fie upon this single life! Forgo it:

---

7   *Misrule* ed. (Misse-rule Q); *Lord of Misrule* (1) Someone very young or of low degree,
    traditionally chosen to preside over feasts and revels at court, reversing the usual
    hierarchies (2) Punning on *Mis* / *misse* = kept mistress. On the retrospectively bittter
    irony of this joke about the Lord of Misrule, see below, note to IV.ii.1.
22   *Never* An ironically prophetic answer: this dialogue recalls *Antony and Cleopatra*,
    I.ii, where the Soothsayer converses with Charmian, Iras and Alexas.

We read how Daphne, for her peevish flight,
Became a fruitless bay-tree, Syrinx turn'd   25
To the pale empty reed, Anaxarete
Was frozen into marble, whereas those
Which married, or proved kind unto their friends,
Were by a gracious influence transshaped
Into the olive, pomegranate, mulberry,   30
Became flowers, precious stones or eminent stars.

CARIOLA

This is a vain poetry; but I pray you tell me,
If there were proposed me wisdom, riches, and beauty,
In three several young men, which should I choose?

ANTONIO

'Tis a hard question. This was Paris' case   35
And he was blind in't, and there was great cause:
For how was't possible he could judge right,
Having three amorous goddesses in view,
And they stark naked? 'Twas a motion
Were able to be-night the apprehension   40
Of the severest counsellor of Europe.
Now I look on both your faces so well formed
It puts me in mind of a question I would ask.

CARIOLA

What is't?

ANTONIO   I do wonder why hard-favoured ladies
For the most part keep worse-favoured waiting-women   45
To attend them, and cannot endure fair ones.

DUCHESS

Oh, that's soon answered.
Did you ever in your life know an ill painter
Desire to have his dwelling next door to the shop
Of an excellent picture-maker? 'Twould disgrace   50
His face-making, and undo him. – I prithee
When were we so merry? My hair tangles.

ANTONIO [*Aside to* CARIOLA]

Pray thee, Cariola, let's steal forth the room

24   *flight* ed. (slight Q1).
25   *Syrinx* ed. (Siriux Q1b, Sirina Q1a).
28   *friends* lovers.
39   *motion* show.
40   *apprehension* Q1b (approbation Q1a).
49   *his* Q1b (the Q1a).

And let her talk to herself. I have divers times
Served her the like, when she hath chafed extremely.   55
I love to see her angry. Softly Cariola.

Exeunt [ANTONIO *and* CARIOLA]

DUCHESS

Doth not the colour of my hair 'gin to change?
When I wax grey I shall have all the court
Powder their hair with arras, to be like me:

[*Enter* FERDINAND, *behind*]

You have cause to love me, I enter'd you into my heart   60
Before you would vouchsafe to call for the keys.
We shall one day have my brothers take you napping:
Methinks his presence, being now in court,
Should make you keep your own bed; but you'll say
Love mixed with fear is sweetest. I'll assure you   65
You shall get no more children till my brothers
Consent to be your gossips. – Have you lost your tongue?

[*She sees* FERDINAND]

'Tis welcome:
For know, whether I am doomed to live, or die,
I can do both like a prince.

FERDINAND *gives her a poniard*

FERDINAND   Die then, quickly!   70
Virtue, where art thou hid? What hideous thing
Is it that doth eclipse thee?

DUCHESS   Pray sir hear me.

FERDINAND

Or is it true thou art but a bare name,
And no essential thing?

56   s.d., 59 s.d. An ironic parallel with I.i.352–464 where, after hiding behind the arras,
     Cariola appears, surprising Antonio. Lucas unpersuasively suggests (in view of line
     145 below) that here Webster intends Ferdinand to be seen crossing the upper stage
     before descending out of sight and then making this entrance on the main stage.
59   *arras* powdered orris-root, white and smelling of violets, used on the hair.
67   *gossips* godparents for the children.
67–8 Q4 (Consent . . . welcome Q1).
67   s.d. The staging is especially powerful if the Duchess catches sight of Ferdinand in
     the mirror. There is a visual allusion to the Dance of Death, where the figure of
     Death arrests men and women of various ages and ranks, including youthful queens
     and duchesses. The mirror in such cases is an emblem of female vanity.
70   ed. (I . . . Prince / Die . . quickle Q1).
70   s.d. Q1b (not in Q1a); *poniard* Presumably the dagger is his father's, the one with
     which he threatened the Duchess in I.i.321.

DUCHESS   Sir –
FERDINAND   Do not speak.
DUCHESS
  No sir: 75
  I will plant my soul in mine ears to hear you.
FERDINAND
  Oh most imperfect light of human reason,
  That mak'st so unhappy to foresee
  What we can least prevent, pursue thy wishes
  And glory in them: there's in shame no comfort   80
  But to be past all bounds and sense of shame.
DUCHESS
  I pray sir, hear me: I am married.
FERDINAND   So.
DUCHESS
  Happily, not to your liking; but for that,
  Alas, your shears do come untimely now
  To clip the bird's wings that's already flown.   85
  Will you see my husband?
FERDINAND   Yes, if I could change
  Eyes with a basilisk.
DUCHESS   Sure, you came hither
  By his confederacy.
FERDINAND   The howling of a wolf
  Is music to thee, screech owl, prithee peace.
  What e'er thou art that hast enjoyed my sister –   90
  For I am sure thou hear'st me – for thine own sake
  Let me not know thee. I came hither prepared
  To work thy discovery, yet am now persuaded
  It would beget such violent effects
  As would damn us both. I would not for ten millions   95
  I had beheld thee, therefore use all means
  I never may have knowledge of thy name.
  Enjoy thy lust still, and a wretched life,
  On that condition; and for thee, vile woman,

---

  83   *Happily* Perhaps.
86–8 ed. (Will . . . Husband / Yes . . . I / Could . . . Basilisque / Sure . . . hither / By . . .
       consideracy / The . . . Wolfe Q1).
  87   *basilisk* a mythical kind of serpent: its breath, or the sight of it, was supposedly fatal.
  88   *confederacy* ed. (consideracy Q1).
  89   *to thee* compared to thee.

If thou do wish thy lecher may grow old   100
In thy embracements, I would have thee build
Such a room for him as our anchorites
To holier use inhabit. Let not the sun
Shine on him till he's dead, let dogs and monkeys
Only converse with him, and such dumb things   105
To whom nature denies use to sound his name.
Do not keep a paraquito lest she learn it.
If thou do love him cut out thine own tongue
Lest it bewray him.
DUCHESS   Why might not I marry?
I have not gone about in this to create   110
Any new world or custom.
FERDINAND   Thou art undone;
And thou hast ta'en that massy sheet of lead
That hid thy husband's bones, and folded it
About my heart.
DUCHESS   Mine bleeds for't.
FERDINAND   Thine? Thy heart?
What should I name't, unless a hollow bullet   115
Filled with unquenchable wild-fire?
DUCHESS   You are in this
Too strict, and were you not my princely brother
I would say too wilful. My reputation
Is safe.
FERDINAND Dost thou know what reputation is?
I'll tell thee – to small purpose, since th'instruction   120
Comes now too late.
Upon a time Reputation, Love, and Death
Would travel o'er the world; and it was concluded
That they should part, and take three several ways:
Death told them they should find him in great battles   125
Or cities plagued with plagues; Love gives them counsel
To enquire for him 'mongst unambitious shepherds,
Where dowries were not talked of, and sometimes
'Mongst quiet kindred that had nothing left
By their dead parents. 'Stay', quoth Reputation,   130

115   *What . . . unless* What else should I call it but.
        hollow bullet cannon-ball filled with explosive, not the older type which was a solid
        iron ball.
118   *too* ed. (to Q1).

'Do not forsake me: for it is my nature
If once I part from any man I meet
I am never found again'; and so for you:
You have shook hands with Reputation
And made him invisible. So fare you well.   135
I will never see you more.
DUCHESS   Why should only I
Of all the other princes of the world
Be cased up like a holy relic? I have youth,
And a little beauty.
FERDINAND   So you have some virgins
That are witches. I will never see thee more.   *Exit*   140

    Enter ANTONIO *with a pistol* [*and* CARIOLA]

DUCHESS
You saw this apparition?
ANTONIO   Yes, we are
Betrayed. How came he hither? I should turn
This to thee, for that.
                              [*Points the pistol at* CARIOLA]
CARIOLA   Pray sir do: and when
That you have cleft my heart you shall read there
Mine innocence.
DUCHESS   That gallery gave him entrance.   145
ANTONIO
I would this terrible thing would come again
That, standing on my guard, I might relate
My warrantable love. Ha, what means this?
DUCHESS
He left this with me –
                              She shows the poniard
ANTONIO   And it seems did wish
You would use it on yourself?

---

134   *shook* Q1c (shooked Q1a, Q1b).
145   *gallery* It is not likely that *gallery* refers to the stage's upper playing space, since
'above' is how the Elizabethans referred to this part of the tiring-house: more
probably it is one of the play's numerous references to specific rooms and parts of
palaces and houses in the named cities – Malfi, Rome, Loreto, Ancona, Milan. As
with IV.ii.31 where the Duchess' portrait is said to hang in the gallery, the effect is
impressionistic rather than exactly realistic in the nineteenth-century manner of
Ibsen.

DUCHESS His action 150
    Seemed to intend so much.

ANTONIO This hath a handle to't
    As well as a point, turn it towards him
    And so fasten the keen edge in his rank gall.

                         [*Knocking*]

    How now? Who knocks? More earthquakes?

DUCHESS I stand
    As if a mine beneath my feet were ready 155
    To be blown up.

CARIOLA 'Tis Bosola.

DUCHESS Away!
    Oh misery, methinks unjust actions
    Should wear these masks and curtains, and not we:
    You must instantly part hence: I have fashioned it already.

                        Exit ANTONIO

        [*Enter* BOSOLA]

BOSOLA
    The Duke your brother is ta'en up in a whirlwind: 160
    Hath took horse and's rid post to Rome.

DUCHESS So late?

BOSOLA
    He told me as he mounted into th'saddle
    You were undone.

DUCHESS Indeed I am very near it.

BOSOLA
    What's the matter?

DUCHESS
    Antonio, the master of our household 165
    Hath dealt so falsely with me in's accounts.
    My brother stood engaged with me for money
    Ta'en up of certain Neapolitan Jews,
    And Antonio lets the bonds be forfeit.

BOSOLA
    Strange! [*Aside*] This is cunning.

DUCHESS And hereupon 170

165–72   A similar feeble excuse, of theft, to that in II.ii.48ff., where Bosola was also present.
  167–8   *stood . . . up* was security for money I borrowed.
     169   *lets . . . forfeit* Presumably by failing to make the payments.

My brother's bills at Naples are protested
Against. Call up our officers.

BOSOLA   I shall.   *Exit*

[*Enter* ANTONIO]

DUCHESS
The place that you must fly to is Ancona:
Hire a house there. I'll send after you
My treasure and my jewels. Our weak safety   175
Runs upon enginous wheels, short syllables
Must stand for periods. I must now accuse you
Of such a feigned crime as Tasso calls
Magnanima mensogna, a noble lie,
'Cause it must shield our honours. Hark, they are coming!   180

[*Enter* BOSOLA *and* OFFICERS]

ANTONIO
Will your grace hear me?

DUCHESS
I have got well by you: you have yielded me
A million of loss; I am like to inherit
The people's curses for your stewardship.
You had the trick in audit time to be sick   185
Till I had signed your *Quietus*; and that cured you
Without help of a doctor. Gentlemen,
I would have this man be an example to you all,
So shall you hold my favour. I pray let him,
For h'as done that, alas, you would not think of,   190
And, because I intend to be rid of him,
I mean not to publish. – Use your fortune elsewhere.

171–2   *bills . . . Against* promissory notes are not accepted.
173   But see below 300–306 and n.
176   *enginous* ed. (engenous Q1).
        enginous wheels Like those of a clock where a small, almost imperceptible movement
        produces obvious motion in the hands (Brennan).
178   *Tasso* Alluding to *Gerusalemme Liberata*, 2.22, where Soprina falsely confesses taking
        a statue of the Virgin Mary from a mosque, in order to prevent wholesale
        persecution of her fellow Christians.
182   *got well* This double entendre is the first of a series down to 207 in which the Duchess
        and Antonio covertly affirm their love. For a memorable instance in Shakespeare
        see *Romeo and Juliet*, III.v.68–102.
189   *let him* let him go free (but *let* could also mean 'stop').

ANTONIO

    I am strongly armed to brook my overthrow,
    As commonly men bear with a hard year.
    I will not blame the cause on't but do think   195
    The necessity of my malevolent star
    Procures this, not her humour. Oh the inconstant
    And rotten ground of service you may see:
    Tis ev'n like him that in a winter night
    Takes a long slumber o'er a dying fire   200
    As loth to part from't, yet parts thence as cold
    As when he first sat down.

DUCHESS   We do confiscate,
    Towards the satisfying of your accounts,
    All that you have.

ANTONIO   I am all yours: and 'tis very fit
    All mine should be so.

DUCHESS   So, sir; you have your pass.   205

ANTONIO

    You may see, gentlemen, what 'tis to serve
    A prince with body and soul.   *Exit*

BOSOLA

    Here's an example for extortion! What moisture is drawn out of
    the sea, when foul weather comes, pours down and runs into
    the sea again.   210

DUCHESS

    I would know what are your opinions of this Antonio.

2 OFFICER

    He could not abide to see a pig's head gaping; I thought your
    grace would find him a Jew.

3 OFFICER

    I would you had been his officer, for your own sake.

4 OFFICER

    You would have had more money.   215

---

    201   *As loth* Q1c (A-loth Q1a, Q1b).
212–23   prose ed. (*Q1 lines ending* gaping / Iew / sake / money / came / hearing / woman / full / goe / him / Chaine).
212–13   *pig's head . . . Jew* A crudely racist way of saying Antonio is financially untrustworthy – the sycophantic Officer takes the hint of line 168's reference to Neapolitan Jews. Webster is again drawing on *Merchant of Venice*: in IV.i Shylock refers twice to one who 'cannot abide a gaping pig'. A Christian proverb is 'Invite not a Jew either to pig or pork' (Tilley P310).

1 OFFICER

He stopped his ears with black wool, and to those came to him
for money, said he was thick of hearing.

2 OFFICER

Some said he was an hermaphrodite, for he could not abide a
woman.

4 OFFICER

How scurvy proud he would look when the treasury was full!   220
Well, let him go.

1 OFFICER

Yes, and the chippings of the butt'ry fly after him, to scour his
gold chain!

DUCHESS

Leave us.

Exeunt [OFFICERS]

[*To* BOSOLA] What do you think of these?

BOSOLA

That these are rogues that, in's prosperity,   225
But to have waited on his fortune, could have wished
His dirty stirrup riveted through their noses
And followed after's mule like a bear in a ring;
Would have prostituted their daughters to his lust,
Made their first born intelligencers, thought none happy   230
But such as were born under his blessed planet
And wore his livery; and do these lice drop off now?
Well, never look to have the like again.
He hath left a sort of flatt'ring rogues behind him:
Their doom must follow. Princes pay flatterers   235
In their own money: flatterers dissemble their vices,
And they dissemble their lies: that's justice.
Alas, poor gentleman.

DUCHESS

Poor? He hath amply filled his coffers.

---

222   *chippings* parings of the crust of a loaf.
223   *gold chain* The steward's official chain of office. In *Twelfth Night*, II.iii.119–20,
       Malvolio is mockingly told to rub his chain 'with crumbs'.
225ff. Bosola's praise of Antonio is an elaborate and over-extended ploy, yet it persuades
       the Duchess to confide in him. Perhaps she is so surprised to hear praise from this
       wonted malcontent that she is disarmed; but even if Bosola's estimation of Antonio
       is sincere, he continues to serve Ferdinand.
230   *intelligencers* Q1c (and intelligencers Q1a, Q1b).

BOSOLA

    Sure he was too honest. Pluto the god of riches,   240
    When he's sent by Jupiter to any man,
    He goes limping, to signify that wealth
    That comes on god's name, comes slowly; but when he's sent
    On the devil's errand he rides post and comes in by scuttles.
    Let me show you what a most unvalued jewel   245
    You have in a wanton humour thrown away
    To bless the man shall find him. He was an excellent
    Courtier, and most faithful, a soldier that thought it
    As beastly to know his own value too little
    As devilish to acknowledge it too much;   250
    Both his virtue and form deserved a far better fortune;
    His discourse rather delighted to judge itself than show itself,
    His breast was filled with all perfection
    And yet it seemed a private whisp'ring room,
    It made so little noise of't.

DUCHESS   But he was basely descended.   255

BOSOLA

    Will you make yourself a mercenary herald,
    Rather to examine men's pedigrees than virtues?
    You shall want him,
    For know: an honest statesman to a prince
    Is like a cedar planted by a spring;   260
    The spring bathes the tree's root, the grateful tree
    Rewards it with his shadow. You have not done so:
    I would sooner swim to the Bermoothes on
    Two politicians' rotten bladders, tied
    Together with an intelligencer's heart-string,   265
    Than depend on so changeable a prince's favour!
    Fare thee well, Antonio: since the malice of the world
    Would needs down with thee, it cannot be said yet
    That any ill happened unto thee,
    Considering thy fall was accompanied with virtue.   270

240   *Pluto* The god of riches was Plutus, whereas Pluto was god of the underworld. Lucas
      suggests that the link of association was that wealth came from underground.
244   *On* ed. (One Q1).
      scuttles The meaning is uncertain: 'short hurried runs' (*OED*) or 'large baskets'
      (Brown).
245   *unvalued* priceless, very valuable.
263   *Bermoothes* The reports of the wreck of Sir George Somers on the Bermudas in 1609
      were topical and famous, and were used by Shakespeare in writing *The Tempest*.

DUCHESS

Oh, you render me excellent music.

BOSOLA   Say you?

DUCHESS

This good one that you speak of is my husband.

BOSOLA

Do I not dream? Can this ambitious age
Have so much goodness in't as to prefer
A man merely for worth, without these shadows   275
Of wealth and painted honours? Possible?

DUCHESS

I have had three children by him.

BOSOLA   Fortunate lady,
For you have made your private nuptial bed
The humble and fair seminary of peace,
No question but many an unbeneficed scholar   280
Shall pray for you, for this deed, and rejoice
That some preferment in the world can yet
Arise from merit. The virgins of your land
That have no dowries, shall hope your example
Will raise them to rich husbands; should you want   285
Soldiers 'twould make the very Turks and Moors
Turn Christians and serve you, for this act;
Last, the neglected poets of your time,
In honour of this trophy of a man
Raised by that curious engine, your white hand,   290
Shall thank you, in your grave, for't, and make that
More reverend than all the cabinets
Of living princes. For Antonio,
His fame shall likewise flow from many a pen
When heralds shall want coats to sell to men.   295

DUCHESS

As I taste comfort in this friendly speech,
So would I find concealment.

BOSOLA

Oh the secret of my prince,
Which I will wear on th'inside of my heart!

290   *curious* delicate, dainty.
295   The sale of honours (involving the devising of coats of arms) was a subject of much
       attack by satirists in the early Jacobean age.

DUCHESS

    You shall take charge of all my coin, and jewels,   300

    And follow him, for he retires himself

    To Ancona.

BOSOLA   So.

DUCHESS   Whither, within few days,

    I mean to follow thee.

BOSOLA   Let me think:

    I would wish your grace to feign a pilgrimage

    To Our Lady of Loreto, scarce seven leagues   305

    From fair Ancona: so may you depart

    Your country with more honour, and your flight

    Will seem a princely progress, retaining

    Your usual train about you.

DUCHESS   Sir, your direction

    Shall lead me by the hand.

CARIOLA   In my opinion   310

    She were better progress to the baths

    At Lucca, or go visit the Spa

    In Germany, for, if you will believe me,

    I do not like this jesting with religion,

    This feigned pilgrimage.   315

DUCHESS

    Thou art a superstitious fool.

    Prepare us instantly for our departure.

    Past sorrows, let us moderately lament them,

    For those to come, seek wisely to prevent them.

                 Exeunt [DUCHESS *and* CARIOLA]

BOSOLA

    A politician is the devil's quilted anvil,   320

    He fashions all sins on him and the blows

    Are never heard – he may work in a lady's chamber,

    As here for proof. What rests, but I reveal

300–6   According to 173 above, Antonio was to go directly to Ancona and by now might be
        supposed to be on the way, but when she changes the plan the Duchess does not
        refer to Antonio; nevertheless in III.iv.6 s.d. Antonio is with her at Loreto. Either
        this is an error by Webster or we are tacitly to assume that Antonio came from
        Ancona to meet her.

309   *usual train* The number of attendants was (and still is) a sign of power and prestige:
        Shakespeare's King Lear requires a hundred knights.

312   *the Spa* In Belgium, a famous watering-place; Webster could have found in
        Montaigne, *Essayes*, II.xv, p. 357, adjacent references to Ancona, Lucca, Loreto and
        Spa.

All to my lord? Oh, this base quality
Of intelligencer! Why, every quality i'th'world   325
Prefers but gain or commendation:
Now for this act I am certain to be raised,
And men that paint weeds – to the life – are praised.   *Exit*

[ACT III,] SCENE iii

[*Enter* CARDINAL, FERDINAND, MALATESTE,
PESCARA, SILVIO, *and* DELIO]

CARDINAL
Must we turn soldier then?
MALATESTE   The Emperor
Hearing your worth that way, ere you attained
This reverend garment, joins you in commission
With the right fortunate soldier, the Marquis of Pescara,
And the famous Lannoy.
CARDINAL   He that had the honour   5
Of taking the French King prisoner?
MALATESTE   The same.
[*Shows plan*] Here's a plot drawn for a new fortification,
At Naples.
FERDINAND This great Count Malateste I perceive
Hath got employment?
DELIO   No employment, my lord,
A marginal note in the muster-book that he is   10
A voluntary lord.
FERDINAND   He's no soldier?
DELIO
He has worn gunpowder in's hollow tooth,

---

326   *Prefers* Assists in bringing about (*OED*).

0   s.d. ed. (*SCENA III. / Cardinall, Ferdinand, Mallateste, Pescara, Silvio, Delio, Bosola. Q1*)
1   *Emperor* Charles V.
3   *reverend garment* the robes of a Cardinal.
5   *famous Lannoy* The historical figure Charles de Lannoy (c.1487–1527) received the
     surrendered sword of Francis I of France at the battle of Pavia in 1525.
7   *plot* ground-plan.

For the tooth-ache.

SILVIO

    He comes to the leaguer with a full intent
    To eat fresh beef and garlic, means to stay   15
    Till the scent be gone, and straight return to court.

DELIO

    He hath read all the late service,
    As the city chronicle relates it,
    And keeps two painters going, only to express
    Battles in model.

SILVIO   Then he'll fight by the book.   20

DELIO

    By the almanac, I think,
    To choose good days and shun the critical. –
    That's his mistress' scarf.

SILVIO   Yes, he protests
    He would do much for that taffeta.

DELIO

    I think he would run away from a battle   25
    To save it from taking prisoner.

SILVIO   He is horribly afraid
    Gunpowder will spoil the perfume on't.

DELIO

    I saw a Dutchman break his pate once
    For calling him pot-gun: he made his head
    Have a bore in't like a musket.   30

SILVIO

    I would he had made a touch-hole to't.

14   *leaguer* army camp.
17   *service* military campaign.
19   *keeps* ed. (keepe Q1).
      painters Q1c (pewterers Q1a-b) 'Press-corrections in this forme are probably authorial' (Brown).
20   *model* drawings made to scale.
      by the book only theoretically. The phrase means 'strictly according to the rules', whether in a good sense or bad – see *Romeo and Juliet*, I.v.110, III.i.102.
29   *pot-gun* a term for a short-barrelled pot-shaped artillery-piece, contemptuously applied to a pistol (OED sb, 2b) or figuratively, as here, to a braggart (OED sb. 3). English dramatists of the period caricature Dutch indulgence in butter and beer.
31   *touch-hole* hole in the breech for igniting the charge.

[DELIO]

He is indeed a guarded sumpter-cloth
Only for the remove of the court.

[*Enter* BOSOLA, *who speaks apart to* FERDINAND
and the CARDINAL]

PESCARA

Bosola arriv'd? What should be the business?
Some falling-out amongst the cardinals.   35
These factions amongst great men, they are like
Foxes: when their heads are divided
They carry fire in their tails, and all the country
About them goes to wrack for't.

SILVIO   What's that Bosola?

DELIO

I knew him in Padua, a fantastical scholar, like such who study   40
to know how many knots was in Hercules' club, of what colour
Achilles' beard was, or whether Hector were not troubled with
the tooth-ache. He hath studied himself half blear-eyed to
know the true symmetry of Caesar's nose by a shoeing-horn,
and this he did to gain the name of a speculative man.   45

PESCARA

Mark Prince Ferdinand,
A very salamander lives in's eye
To mock the eager violence of fire.

SILVIO

That Cardinal hath made more bad faces with his oppression
than ever Michael Angelo made good ones; he lifts up's nose   50
like a foul porpoise before a storm.

PESCARA

The Lord Ferdinand laughs.

32   DELIO *He* ed. (He Q1) The catchword at the bottom of the preceding page, G4v, is
      Del. NCW suggest the omission of the s.p. occurred because the compositor went
      from G4v to the inner forme of H (H1v and H2r) before returning to H1r, when he
      overlooked it.
      guarded sumpter-cloth ornamented cloth covering a pack-horse or mule.
37–8 Alluding to Judges 15.4, the trick of Samson who tied pairs of foxes together by their
      tails, attached firebrands to them, and sent them into the Philistines' crops to destroy
      them.
40–5 prose ed. (*Q1 lines ending* scholler / in / was / – ach / the / this / man).
47   *salamander* supposed to live in fire, the element of passion, destruction or torment.
49–51 prose ed (*Q1 lines ending* oppression / ones / storme).
51   *porpoise* (por-pisse Q1)..

DELIO   Like a deadly cannon
  That lightens ere it smokes.
PESCARA
  These are your true pangs of death,
  The pangs of life that struggle with great statesmen.   55
DELIO
  In such a deformed silence witches whisper their charms.
CARDINAL
  Doth she make religion her riding-hood
  To keep her from the sun, and tempest?
FERDINAND   That –
  That damns her: Methinks her fault and beauty,
  Blended together, show like leprosy,   60
  The whiter, the fouler: I make it a question
  Whether her beggarly brats were ever christened.
CARDINAL
  I will instantly solicit the state of Ancona
  To have them banished.
FERDINAND   You are for Loreto?
  I shall not be at your ceremony: fare you well.   65
  [*To* BOSOLA] Write to the Duke of Malfi, my young nephew
  She had by her first husband, and acquaint him
  With's mother's honesty.
BOSOLA   I will.
FERDINAND   Antonio?
  A slave that only smelled of ink and counters,
  And ne'er in's life looked like a gentleman   70
  But in the audit time! Go, go presently,
  Draw me out an hundred and fifty of our horse,
  And meet me at the fort bridge.

                                                          Exeunt

---

56–60   ed. (In . . . charmes / Doth . . . hood / To . . . tempest / That . . . and / Beauty . . .
        leaprosie Q1).

66–7   This is the only reference to this son. Perhaps he is a 'ghost character' from an early
        draft whom Webster forgot to delete. His existence seems incompatible with
        Ferdinand's hope at IV.ii.269–71 of inheriting a mass of treasure at the Duchess'
        death.

69   *counters* small discs used in accounting.

70   *life* ed. (like Q1).

72   *hundred* ed. (hundreth Q1).

[ACT III,] SCENE iv

[Enter] TWO PILGRIMS *to the shrine*
of Our Lady of Loretto

1 PILGRIM
I have not seen a goodlier shrine than this,
Yet I have visited many.

2 PILGRIM   The Cardinal of Aragon
Is this day to resign his cardinal's hat,
His sister Duchess likewise is arrived
To pay her vow of pilgrimage. I expect   5
A noble ceremony.

1 PILGRIM   No question. – They come.

Here the ceremony of the Cardinal's instalment
in the habit of a soldier: performed in delivering up
his cross, hat, robes and ring, at the shrine; and investing
him with sword, helmet, shield, and spurs: then ANTONIO,
the DUCHESS *and their children, having presented themselves*
at the shrine, are by a form of banishment in dumb-show,
expressed towards them by the CARDINAL *and the*
State of Ancona, banished; during all which ceremony,
this ditty is sung to very solemn music, by divers churchmen;
and then

Exeunt.

0   s.d. ed. (SCENA IIII. / Two Pilgrimes to the Shrine of our Lady of Loreto. Q1).

0   s.d. 1 PILGRIMS The traditional dress of a pilgrim consisted of a gown, staff, scallop-shell, scrip and bottle, as described in Sir Walter Raleigh's poem 'The passionate man's Pilgrimage'.

0   s.d. 1 *shrine* The actual Loreto shrine featured a black madonna with child, and Webster may have intended an elaborate imitation, a spectacle composing a pattern with the later spectacular staging of the bodies (IV.i) and the tomb (V.iii).

6   s.d. 2 *habit* Q1b (*order* Q1a); *of a* ed. (*a* Q1).
     s.d. 5 *children* A boy, a girl old enough to say her prayers (see IV.ii.191–2) and a babe in arms.

6   s.d. 6 *in dumb-show* Q1b (not in Q1a). This dumb-show must include the violent removal of the wedding-ring from the finger of the Duchess, as lines 35–6 indicate. The dumb-show signals a decisive turning point with the Cardinal's transformation into soldier and the simultaneous subjection suffered by the Duchess. The presence of Antonio seems to contradict III.ii.173 where the Duchess tells him to go to Ancona. See above, III.ii.300–306 n.

6   s.d. 9 *ditty* Q1b (*Hymne* Q1a).

Arms, and honours, deck thy story
To thy fame's eternal glory,
Adverse fortune ever fly thee,
No disastrous fate come nigh thee.   The author   10
                                                      disclaims
I alone will sing thy praises,   this ditty
Whom to honour, virtue raises;   to be his
And thy study, that divine is,
Bent to martial discipline is.
Lay aside all those robes lie by thee,   15
Crown thy arts with arms: they'll beautify thee.

Oh worthy of worthiest name, adorned in this manner,
Lead bravely thy forces on, under war's warlike banner:
Oh mayest thou prove fortunate in all martial courses,
Guide thou still, by skill, in arts and forces: 20
Victory attend thee nigh whilst fame sings loud thy powers,
Triumphant conquest crown thy head, and blessings pour down
    showers.

1 PILGRIM
  Here's a strange turn of state: who would have thought
  So great a lady would have matched herself
  Unto so mean a person? Yet the Cardinal   25
  Bears himself much too cruel.
2 PILGRIM   They are banished.
1 PILGRIM
  But I would ask what power hath this state
  Of Ancona to determine of a free prince?
2 PILGRIM
  They are a free state sir, and her brother showed
  How that the Pope, forehearing of her looseness,   30

---

7   *Arms* Q1b (The Hymne. / *Armes* Q1a) (but the catch-word in Q1b is not corrected
     and reads 'The').
10–13 *The . . . his* Q1b (opposite line 3 on sig H2r – not in Q1a). Added, presumably by
     Webster, when the text was read in proof. The author of the ditty has not been
     identified.
19   *courses* encounters.
29   *free state* Ancona had been an independent republic but by Webster's time was one
     of the Papal States, and as 2 Pilgrim explains, this gives the Cardinal an excuse to act
     ostensibly in the name of the Papacy to gain his revenge.
     state sir Q1b (state Q1).

Hath seized into the protection of the Church
The dukedom which she held as dowager.

1 PILGRIM
But by what justice?

2 PILGRIM   Sure I think by none,
Only her brother's instigation.

1 PILGRIM
What was it with such violence he took   35
Off from her finger?

2 PILGRIM   'Twas her wedding ring,
Which he vowed shortly he would sacrifice
To his revenge.

1 PILGRIM   Alas, Antonio,
If that a man be thrust into a well,
No matter who sets hand to't, his own weight   40
Will bring him sooner to th'bottom. Come, let's hence.
Fortune makes this conclusion general,
'All things do help th'unhappy man to fall'.

                               Exeunt

[ACT III,] SCENE v

[*Enter* ANTONIO, DUCHESS, CHILDREN,
CARIOLA, *and* SERVANTS]

DUCHESS
Banished Ancona?

ANTONIO   Yes, you see what power
Lightens in great men's breath.

---

31   *Hath* Q1b (Had Q1a).
36   *Off* ed. (Of Q1).

0   s.d. ed. (*SCENA V. / Antonio, Duchesse, Children, Cariola, Seruants, Bosola, Souldiers, with Vizards. Q1*).
0   s.d. 1 CARIOLA As line 81 indicates, Cariola has the baby in her arms.
1–3   ed. (Banish'd *Ancona* / Yes ... powre / Lightens ... breath / Is ... traine / Shrunke . .. remainder / These ... men Q1).
2   *Lightens* An intransitive verb, 'flashes like lightning' – as at III.iii.53.

DUCHESS   Is all our train
Shrunk to this poor remainder?
ANTONIO   These poor men,
Which have got little in your service, vow
To take your fortune; but your wiser buntings,   5
Now they are fledged, are gone.
DUCHESS   They have done wisely.
This puts me in mind of death: physicians thus,
With their hands full of money, use to give o'er
Their patients.
ANTONIO   Right the fashion of the world:
From decayed fortunes every flatterer shrinks,   10
Men cease to build where the foundation sinks.
DUCHESS
I had a very strange dream tonight.
ANTONIO   What was't?
DUCHESS
Methought I wore my coronet of state,
And on a sudden all the diamonds
Were changed to pearls.
ANTONIO   My interpretation   15
Is, you'll weep shortly, for to me the pearls
Do signify your tears.
DUCHESS   The birds that live i'th'field
On the wild benefit of nature, live
Happier than we; for they may choose their mates
And carol their sweet pleasures to the spring.   20

[*Enter* BOSOLA *with a letter
which he presents to the* DUCHESS]

BOSOLA
You are happily o'er-ta'en.
DUCHESS   From my brother?
BOSOLA
Yes, from the Lord Ferdinand your brother,
All love, and safety.

5   *buntings* small birds related to the lark but without their song: here applied to the
     servants who have had the wit to see that it is time to leave and have the means to
     do so.
9   *Right* Just.
18   *benefit* gift.

85

DUCHESS   Thou dost blanch mischief,
    Wouldst make it white. See, see, like to calm weather
    At sea before a tempest, false hearts speak fair   25
    To those they intend most mischief.
    [*Reads*] *Send Antonio to me, I want his head in a business –*
    A politic equivocation:
    He doth not want your counsel but your head:
    That is, he cannot sleep till you be dead;   30
    And here's another pitfall that's strewed o'er
    With roses: mark it, 'tis a cunning one:
    [*Reads*] *I stand engaged for your husband, for several debts, at*
       Naples; let not that trouble him, I had rather have his heart
       than his money.   35
    And I believe so too.
BOSOLA   What do you believe?
DUCHESS
    That he so much distrusts my husband's love
    He will by no means believe his heart is with him
    Until he see it. The devil is not cunning enough
    To circumvent us in riddles.   40
BOSOLA
    Will you reject that noble and free league
    Of amity and love which I present you?
DUCHESS
    Their league is like that of some politic kings
    Only to make themselves of strength and power
    To be our after-ruin: tell them so.   45
BOSOLA
    And what from you?
ANTONIO   Thus tell him: I will not come.
BOSOLA
    And what of this?
ANTONIO   My brothers have dispersed
    Bloodhounds abroad; which till I hear are muzzled,
    No truce, though hatched with ne'er such politic skill,
    Is safe, that hangs upon our enemies' will.   50

33–5   This was the (invented) reason the Duchess gave for dismissing Antonio at III.ii.165–9.
       Presumably Bosola, who was present then, reported it like a dutiful spy.
33   s.d. Q4 (A Letter Q1).
37–8   Dent compares Donne, *Ignatius*, 89.
47   *brothers* i.e. brothers-in-law.

I'll not come at them.
BOSOLA   This proclaims your breeding.
Every small thing draws a base mind to fear
As the adamant draws iron. Fare you well sir,
You shall shortly hear from's.   *Exit*
DUCHESS   I suspect some ambush:
Therefore by all my love I do conjure you   55
To take your eldest son and fly towards Milan;
Let us not venture all this poor remainder
In one unlucky bottom.
ANTONIO   You counsel safely:
Best of my life, farewell; since we must part
Heaven hath a hand in't; but no other wise   60
Than as some curious artist takes in sunder
A clock, or watch, when it is out of frame,
To bring't in better order.
DUCHESS   I know not which is best,
To see you dead, or part with you: farewell boy,
Thou art happy that thou hast not understanding   65
To know thy misery; for all our wit
And reading brings us to a truer sense
Of sorrow. In the eternal Church, sir,
I do hope we shall not part thus.
ANTONIO   Oh, be of comfort.
Make patience a noble fortitude,   70
And think not how unkindly we are used:
'Man, like to cassia, is proved best, being bruised'.
DUCHESS
Must I like to a slave-born Russian
Account it praise to suffer tyranny?

53   *adamant* magnet.
57–8   *venture . . . bottom* Alluding to the proverb, 'Venture not all in one bottom' i.e. do not
       risk all your wealth in one ship.
64   *boy* Addressing her son.
68   *the eternal Church* The congregation of the saved in Heaven. The phrase occurs in
       Sidney, *Arcadia* (*Works* I. 233), one of a small cluster of borrowings at this point by
       Webster from Sidney.
72   '*Man* Q1b (Man Q1a).
72   *bruised*' ed. (bruiz'd Q1a, Q1b).
73–4   From Sidney, *Astrophil and Stella*, Sonnet 2: 'and now like slave-borne *Muscovite* / I
       call it praise to suffer Tyrannie'. *Astrophil and Stella* would have become even better
       known after it was included with the *Arcadia* in editions from 1598 on – see William
       A. Ringler Jr., ed. *The Poems of Sir Philip Sidney*, 1962, p. lxii.

And yet, oh heaven, thy heavy hand is in't.   75
I have seen my little boy oft scourge his top
And compared myself to't: nought made me e'er
Go right but heaven's scourge-stick.
ANTONIO   Do not weep:
Heaven fashioned us of nothing; and we strive
To bring ourselves to nothing. Farewell Cariola   80
And thy sweet armful. –
[*To* DUCHESS]   If I do never see thee more,
Be a good mother to your little ones,
And save them from the tiger. Fare you well.
DUCHESS
Let me look upon you once more: for that speech
Came from a dying father. Your kiss is colder   85
Than that I have seen an holy anchorite
Give to a dead man's skull.
ANTONIO
My heart is turned to a heavy lump of lead,
With which I sound my danger: fare you well.
                              Exit [*with his eldest son*]
DUCHESS
My laurel is all withered.   90
CARIOLA
Look, madam, what a troop of armed men
Make toward us.

76–8   Compare Sidney, *Arcadia* (*Works* I. 227): 'Griefe onely makes his wretched state to
        see / (Even like a toppe which nought but whipping moves)'.
77–8   ed. (And . . . right / But . . . -sticke / Doe . . . weepe Q1).
  78   *scourge-stick* whip used to make a child's top spin.
79–80   Lucas compares Donne, *An Anatomy of the World*, lines 155–7, but Donne's 'God' has
        been altered to 'Heaven'. A Jacobean statute (3 Jac. I) forbade profanities; and this has
        been thought to explain the substitution. Brown observes (pp.lxviii-lxix) that in the
        play's other instances 'heaven' refers to the skies or the heavenly world and is not
        plausible as a substitution for an original 'God'; moreover it is the fact of a complete
        absence of oaths involving 'God' which is strange in Q1 and strongly suggests
        censorship.
  81   *sweet armful* The Duchess' youngest child.
        never see thee more The phrase is an echo of III.ii.140 and recurs at IV.i.24 and
        V.iii.41.
  86   *anchorite* hermit.
88–9   As the depth of water is gauged (*sounded*) with a lead-weighted line, so the weight
        of Antonio's heavy heart can sound the danger.
  90   An ominous sign, referred to in Shakespeare, *Richard II*, II.iv.7–8.

[*Enter* BOSOLA *with a guard with vizards*]

DUCHESS   Oh they are very welcome:
When Fortune's wheel is overcharged with princes
The weight makes it move swift. I would have my ruin
Be sudden. [*To* BOSOLA] I am your adventure, am I not?   95

BOSOLA
You are. You must see your husband no more.

DUCHESS
What devil art thou that counterfeits heaven's thunder?

BOSOLA
Is that terrible? I would have you tell me
Whether is that note worse that frights the silly birds
Out of the corn, or that which doth allure them   100
To the nets? You have harkened to the last too much.

DUCHESS
Oh misery: like to a rusty o'er-charged cannon,
Shall I never fly in pieces? Come: to what prison?

BOSOLA
To none.

DUCHESS   Whither then?

BOSOLA   To your palace.

DUCHESS
I have heard that Charon's boat serves to convey   105
All o'er the dismal lake, but brings none back again.

BOSOLA
Your brothers mean you safety and pity.

DUCHESS   Pity?

92   s.d. The use of masks by the soldiers, and Bosola, is menacing. The play contains many textual references to disguise and masks, reinforced in visual terms by this episode, by the stage presentation of a masque of madmen, and Bosola's various disguises.

94   *move* Q1b (more Q1a).

95   *I am your adventure* I am your target (but possibly in an ironic sense, 'You aim to find me as if by chance').

98   s.p. Q1b (not in Q1a).

99   *silly* weak, defenceless.

101   s.p. Q1b (*Ant.* Q1a).

102   *o'er-charged* ed. (ore-char'd Q1).

102–3   The image is used for the soul leaving the body at death by Donne, *Of the Progress of the Soul: The Second Anniversary*, lines 181–2.

105   *Charon's boat* In Classical mythology Charon was the ferryman who conveyed the dead across the river Styx to Hades.

107–8   ed. (Your . . . pitie / Pitie. . . aliue Q1).

With such a pity men preserve alive
Pheasants and quails, when they are not fat enough
To be eaten.

BOSOLA   These are your children?

DUCHESS   Yes.

BOSOLA   Can they prattle?

DUCHESS   No: 110
But I intend, since they were born accursed,
Curses shall be their first language.

BOSOLA   Fie, madam,
Forget this base, low fellow.

DUCHESS   Were I a man
I'd beat that counterfeit face into thy other.

BOSOLA
One of no birth.

DUCHESS   Say that he was born mean: 115
Man is most happy when's own actions
Be arguments and examples of his virtue.

BOSOLA
A barren, beggarly virtue.

DUCHESS
I prithee who is greatest, can you tell?
Sad tales befit my woe: I'll tell you one.   120
A salmon as she swam unto the sea
Met with a dog-fish who encounters her
With this rough language: 'Why art thou so bold
To mix thyself with our high state of floods,
Being no eminent courtier, but one   125
That for the calmest and fresh time o'th'year
Dost live in shallow rivers, rank'st thyself
With silly smelts and shrimps? And darest thou
Pass by our dog-ship without reverence?'
'Oh', quoth the salmon, 'sister be at peace: 130
Thank Jupiter we both have passed the net,
Our value never can be truly known
Till in the fisher's basket we be shown.
I'th'market then my price may be the higher

108   *a* Q1b (*not in* Q1a).
110   ed. (To . . . eaten / These . . . children / Yes / Can . . . prattle / No Q1).
112–3   ed. (Curses . . . language / Fye Madam / Forget . . . -fellow / Were . . . man Q1).
114   *counterfeit face* vizard.

Even when I am nearest to the cook, and fire'.   135
So to great men the moral may be stretched:
'Men oft are valued high, when th'are most wretched'.
But come, whither you please: I am armed 'gainst misery,
Bent to all sways of the oppressor's will.
'There's no deep valley, but near some great hill'.   140

Exeunt

ACT IV, SCENE i

[*Enter* FERDINAND, BOSOLA, *and* SERVANTS *with torches*]

FERDINAND
How doth our sister Duchess bear herself
In her imprisonment?

BOSOLA   Nobly; I'll describe her:
She's sad, as one long used to't, and she seems
Rather to welcome the end of misery
Than shun it: a behaviour so noble   5
As gives a majesty to adversity:
You may discern the shape of loveliness
More perfect in her tears than in her smiles;
She will muse four hours together, and her silence,
Methinks, expresseth more than if she spake.   10

FERDINAND
Her melancholy seems to be fortified
With a strange disdain.

BOSOLA   'Tis so: and this restraint,
Like English mastiffs that grow fierce with tying,
Makes her too passionately apprehend

---

0   s.d. ed. (ACTVS IIII. SCENA. I. / Ferdinand, Bosola, Dutchesse, Cariola, Seruants.
     Q1).

0   s.d. Torches and candles, brought on stage, would indicate that this is a night-scene
     (see line 24).

2   *imprisonment* This presumably means (for the moment at least) house-arrest, since
     in III.v.104 Bosola tells the Duchess she is to be taken to her palace not some prison;
     but she may be imagined as moved to a dungeon for her killing (see IV.ii.11 and n.).
     There is a general parallel between the fate of the Duchess and the royal figure of
     Richard II in Shakespeare, except that Webster's Duchess is brought not at once but
     by progressive degrees to mortification: here she is still dressed with the dignity
     proper to her rank, but Bosola commands (IV.i.115ff.) that she is to wear a
     penitential garment next her skin and have beads and a prayer-book, and this may
     indicate how she is to appear in the next scene – her last – IV.ii.

3–5 From Sidney, *Arcadia* (*Works* I. 332).

5–6 Taken from Sidney, *Arcadia* (*Works* I. 16): 'a behaviour so noble, as gave a majestie
     to adversitie'.

7–8 The cadence is close to Sidney, *Arcadia* (*Works* I. 333): 'perceyve the shape of
     lovelinesse more perfectly in wo, then in joyfulnesse' – and Webster's words also
     recall *King Lear*, IV.iii.16–22.

9   *four hours* A common expression for 'several hours' as in *Hamlet*, 2.2.160.

12–15 From Sidney, *Arcadia* (*Works* I. 25).

Those pleasures she's kept from.

FERDINAND   Curse upon her: 15
I will no longer study in the book
Of another's heart: inform her what I told you.   *Exit*

[*Enter* DUCHESS *and* CARIOLA]

BOSOLA
All comfort to your grace.

DUCHESS   I will have none:
Pray thee, why dost thou wrap thy poisoned pills
In gold and sugar?   20

BOSOLA
Your elder brother the Lord Ferdinand
Is come to visit you, and sends you word,
'Cause once he rashly made a solemn vow
Never to see you more, he comes i'th'night:
And prays you, gently, neither torch nor taper   25
Shine in your chamber. He will kiss your hand
And reconcile himself, but, for his vow,
He dares not see you.

DUCHESS   At his pleasure:
Take hence the lights.

[*Exeunt* SERVANTS *with torches*]

[*Enter* FERDINAND]

                   He's come.

FERDINAND
Where are you?

DUCHESS   Here, sir.

FERDINAND   This darkness suits you well.   30

DUCHESS
I would ask you pardon.

FERDINAND   You have it;
For I account it the honorabl'st revenge,

---

21   *elder brother* Since in IV.ii.253 Ferdinand declares he is her twin, here presumably
       Bosola must be supposed mistaken, or to mean that Ferdinand was the first twin to
       be born, or Webster is being careless.

24   *i'th'night* Conventionally indicated on the Elizabethan stage by the bringing on of
       torches or candles.

28–9   ed. (He . . . you / At . . . pleasure / Take . . . come Q1).

30–31   ed. (Where . . . you / Here sir / This . . . well / I . . . pardon / You . . . it Q1).

Where I may kill, to pardon. Where are your cubs?
DUCHESS
Whom?
FERDINAND Call them your children;
For though our national law distinguish bastards   35
From true legitimate issue, compassionate nature
Makes them all equal.
DUCHESS   Do you visit me for this?
You violate a sacrament o'th'Church
Shall make you howl in hell for't.
FERDINAND   It had been well
Could you have lived thus always, for indeed   40
You were too much i'th'light. But no more.
I come to seal my peace with you. Here's a hand
To which you have vowed much love: the ring upon't
You gave.

Gives her a dead man's hand

DUCHESS   I affectionately kiss it.
FERDINAND
Pray do, and bury the print of it in your heart.   45
I will leave this ring with you for a love token,
And the hand, as sure as the ring; and do not doubt
But you shall have the heart too. When you need a friend
Send it to him that owned it: you shall see
Whether he can aid you.
DUCHESS   You are very cold.   50
I fear you are not well after your travel –
Ha? Lights! – Oh horrible!
FERDINAND   Let her have lights enough.   *Exit*

[*Enter* SERVANTS *with torches*]

---

33   *cubs* The first touch of the Duke's future lycanthropia? (Lucas).

41   *i'th'light* in the public eye (and with a play upon *light* = wanton).

43   *the ring upon't* Recalling I.i.405 when the Duchess put a ring on Antonio's finger. In
most productions until the twentieth century the dead man's hand was not used –
in 1850 it was Ferdinand's own 'cold hand' which was kissed. In the 1980 production
the shocked Duchess threw the horribly realistic hand into the audience. (PinP,
p. 151).

44   The Duchess assumes it is Ferdinand's own hand. Her concerned reaction that he
feels cold shows by the starkest contrast how cruel and perverse he has become. M.
C. Bradbrook, MLR (1947), 283–94, points out that, ironically, a dead man's hand
was a charm supposed to cure madness.

DUCHESS

What witchcraft doth he practise, that he hath left
A dead man's hand here?

*Here is discovered behind a traverse the artificial figures
of* ANTONIO *and his children, appearing
as if they were dead.*

BOSOLA

Look you, here's the piece from which 'twas ta'en.   55
He doth present you this sad spectacle,
That now you know directly they are dead.
Hereafter you may, wisely, cease to grieve
For that which cannot be recovered.

DUCHESS

There is not between heaven and earth one wish   60
I stay for after this: it wastes me more
Than were't my picture, fashioned out of wax,
Stuck with a magical needle, and then buried
In some foul dung-hill; and yond's an excellent property
For a tyrant, which I would account mercy.

BOSOLA   What's that?   65

DUCHESS

If they would bind me to that lifeless trunk
And let me freeze to death.

BOSOLA   Come, you must live.

DUCHESS

That's the greatest torture souls feel in hell,
In hell: that they must live, and cannot die.

54   s.d. *traverse* A curtain drawn back to discover the tableau. This spectacle of the dead
      bodies of Antonio and the children is the severest test of the Duchess' sanity and
      faith. Fifty-five lines later, Webster allows the audience (but not the Duchess) to
      learn that these figures were waxwork not real. In Jacobean performances they could,
      as with the stone statue *The Winter's Tale*, have been represented by real actors and
      this would have been the simplest method, the audience taking their cue from the
      Duchess and accepting the figures as dead. Webster makes a point about the
      deceptive illusionism of theatre: the identical theatrical sign can be treacherously
      unstable, can be interpreted in opposite ways. Lopez, p. 109, compares George F.
      Reynolds' view in *The Staging of Elizabethan Plays at the Red Bull Theatre*, p. 40, that
      Elizabethan playwrights 'did, at least in some particulars, delight in realism to an
      extraordinary degree'.
66   In emblem books the image of a live person bound to a corpse symbolised ill-
      matched marriages, but the Duchess characteristically defies commonplace
      attitudes, outfacing horror with her love for her husband: perhaps she moves
      towards the corpse and is restrained by Bosola.

Portia, I'll new kindle thy coals again   70
And revive the rare and almost dead example
Of a loving wife.

BOSOLA   Oh fie: despair? Remember
You are a Christian.

DUCHESS   The Church enjoins fasting:
I'll starve myself to death.

BOSOLA   Leave this vain sorrow.
Things being at the worst, begin to mend: 75
The bee, when he hath shot his sting into your hand,
May then play with your eye-lid.

DUCHESS   Good comfortable fellow,
Persuade a wretch that's broke upon the wheel
To have all his bones new set: entreat him live,
To be executed again. Who must dispatch me?   80
I account this world a tedious theatre,
For I do play a part in't 'gainst my will.

BOSOLA
Come, be of comfort, I will save your life.

DUCHESS
Indeed I have not leisure to tend so small a business.

BOSOLA
Now, by my life, I pity you.

DUCHESS   Thou art a fool then,   85
To waste thy pity on a thing so wretch'd
As cannot pity itself. I am full of daggers –
Puff – let me blow these vipers from me.
[*To a* SERVANT] What are you?

SERVANT   One that wishes you long life.

---

    70   *Portia* Brutus' wife, who choked herself by putting live coals in her mouth after
         hearing of her husband's defeat and death at Philippi.
  81–2   From Sidney, *Arcadia* (*Works* I. 333) and see *Richard II*, V.ii.23–5 where York
         describes the deposed king: 'As in a theatre the eyes of men, / After a well-graced
         actor leaves the stage, /Are idly bent on him that enters next, / Thinking his prattle
         to be tedious'.
    87   *itself* ed. (it Q1).
    88   *vipers* Q1 (vapours Brown). Brown supposes the scribe misread ms 'vapors'.
         let . . . me let me blow away these poisonous thoughts. The pressure of emotion
         transforms the Duchess' metaphor as she speaks: the daggers become the stings of
         snakes (a supplementary image of stinging pain) which she would blow off (as if
         they were burrs).
  89–91 *What . . . me* From Sidney, *Arcadia* (*Works* I. 485).

DUCHESS

    I would thou wert hanged for the horrible curse   90
    Thou hast given me! I shall shortly grow one
    Of the miracles of pity. I'll go pray – no,
    I'll go curse.

BOSOLA   Oh fie.

DUCHESS   I could curse the stars.

BOSOLA   Oh fearful!

DUCHESS

    And those three smiling seasons of the year
    Into a Russian winter, nay the world   95
    To its first chaos.

BOSOLA

    Look you, the stars shine still.

DUCHESS   Oh, but you must
    Remember, my curse hath a great way to go.
    Plagues, that make lanes through largest families,
    Consume them.

BOSOLA   Fie, lady:

DUCHESS   Let them like tyrants   100
    Never be remembered but for the ill they have done:
    Let all the zealous prayers of mortified
    Churchmen forget them.

BOSOLA   Oh uncharitable.

DUCHESS

    Let heaven a little while cease crowning martyrs
    To punish them.   105
    Go howl them this and say I long to bleed:
    'It is some mercy, when men kill with speed'.

                Exeunt [DUCHESS *and* CARIOLA]

              [*Enter* FERDINAND]

FERDINAND

    Excellent, as I would wish, she's plagued in art.
    These presentations are but framed in wax
    By the curious master in that quality,   110
    Vincentio Lauriola, and she takes them

---

99   *make lanes* As does a cannon-ball through a formation of troops in battle.
      them the brothers.

108   Ferdinand has evidently watched and heard everything from concealment, a solitary
      voyeur.

110   *curious* ingenious.

For true substantial bodies.

BOSOLA   Why do you do this?

FERDINAND

To bring her to despair.

BOSOLA   Faith, end here

And go no farther in your cruelty.

Send her a penitential garment to put on   115

Next to her delicate skin, and furnish her

With beads and prayer books.

FERDINAND   Damn her, that body of hers,

While that my blood ran pure in't, was more worth

Than that which thou wouldst comfort, called a soul.

I will send her masques of common courtesans,   120

Have her meat served up by bawds and ruffians,

And, 'cause she'll needs be mad, I am resolved

To remove forth the common hospital

All the mad-folk and place them near her lodging;

There let them practise together, sing and dance   125

And act their gambols to the full o'th'moon.

If she can sleep the better for it, let her.

Your work is almost ended.

BOSOLA

Must I see her again?

FERDINAND   Yes.

BOSOLA   Never.

FERDINAND   You must.

BOSOLA

Never in mine own shape,   130

That's forfeited by my intelligence

And this last cruel lie. When you send me next

The business shall be comfort.

FERDINAND   Very likely.

Thy pity is nothing of kin to thee. Antonio

Lurks about Milan, thou shalt shortly thither   135

To feed a fire as great as my revenge,

115–17   See below, note to IV.ii.0 s.d.
131   *intelligence* spying.
133   *Very likely* This is said and meant ironically – a small touch by which Webster stresses that Ferdinand does not detect the growing crisis in Bosola's personality, the split between cynicism and compassion.

Which ne'er will slack till it have spent his fuel:
'Intemperate agues make physicians cruel'.

Exeunt

[ACT IV,] SCENE ii

[*Enter* DUCHESS *and* CARIOLA]

DUCHESS
What hideous noise was that?

CARIOLA   'Tis the wild consort
Of madmen, lady, which your tyrant brother
Hath placed about your lodging; this tyranny
I think was never practised till this hour.

0   s.d. ed. (*SCENA II. / Duchesse, Cariola, Seruant, Mad-men, Bosola, Executioners,
     Ferdinand. Q1*).

0   s.d. The Duchess may be dressed as a penitent (see IV.i.115–7). Brennan notes that
     ecclesiastical courts sentenced adulteresses to walk through the streets in a
     penitential garment of white, with hair unbound and carrying a lighted taper. Jane
     Shore appears thus in Heywood's play of 1599, *The Second Part of King Edward the
     Fourth*. It is not clear whether in line 11 ('this is a prison') the Duchess is saying that
     she finds her loss of liberty generally depressing, or that she has been moved to an
     actual prison – which would be something very ominous, a suitable place for a
     killing, as in Shakespeare's *Richard II*. In Webster's time such a location would be left
     to the imagination of the spectators, perhaps aided by simple props.

1   *consort* company – with a play on the sense 'group of musicians' – and there may be
     play on *noise* which also could mean 'group of musicians'. Webster may have thus
     intended to alert his audience to the parodies of a Jacobean court wedding masque
     and of a charivari (a mock-masque baiting the bride who married too soon after the
     death of her husband, or who made an unequal match: or a ruffianly band showed
     their disapproval by making clamour and antic dances). The anti-masque precisely
     inverted, in grotesque manner, the harmonies and costly elegance of the main
     masque, in music, words, dance and costume. The Lord of Misrule (see III.ii.7 and
     note) presided at feasts and was chosen for his youth or low degree, inverting the
     normal hierarchy in the spirit of foolery, festive licence and anarchy. See Inga-Stina
     Ekeblad, 'The 'impure art' of John Webster', *RES* 9, (1958), 253–67, who argues that
     the masque of Madmen in IV.ii is related to the charivari. Brown (p.xxxvi) makes a
     connection with actual masques of 1613, Campion's *Lords' Masque* and Beaumont's
     Masque of the Inner Temple and Gray's Inn.
        More broadly, the use of masks in festivals is an ancient tradition formalised in
     comedy, where the temporary release from fixed, normal identity by wearing
     disguise, often in the form of fantastic masks, liberates repressed energies and effects
     positive transformation. Shakespeare gives concentrated attention to these elements
     in *Twelfth Night*, which is occasionally in Webster's mind in this play.

DUCHESS

    Indeed I thank him: nothing but noise and folly   5
    Can keep me in my right wits, whereas reason
    And silence make me stark mad. Sit down,
    Discourse to me some dismal tragedy.

CARIOLA

    Oh 'twill increase your melancholy.

DUCHESS   Thou art deceived,

    To hear of greater grief would lessen mine.   10
    This is a prison?

CARIOLA   Yes, but you shall live

    To shake this durance off.

DUCHESS   Thou art a fool,

    The robin redbreast and the nightingale
    Never live long in cages.

CARIOLA   Pray dry your eyes.

    What think you of, madam?

DUCHESS   Of nothing: 15

    When I muse thus, I sleep.

CARIOLA

    Like a madman, with your eyes open?

DUCHESS

    Dost thou think we shall know one another
    In th'other world?

CARIOLA   Yes, out of question.

DUCHESS

    Oh that it were possible we might   20
    But hold some two days conference with the dead,
    From them I should learn somewhat I am sure
    I never shall know here. I'll tell thee a miracle,
    I am not mad yet, to my cause of sorrow.
    Th'heaven o'er my head seems made of molten brass,   25
    The earth of flaming sulphur, yet I am not mad;
    I am acquainted with sad misery
    As the tanned galley-slave is with his oar.
    Necessity makes me suffer constantly,
    And custom makes it easy. Who do I look like now?   30

---

11   At Blackfriars and the Globe simple props such as chains and fetters could have been
       enough to suggest a prison cell.

15–17   ed. (What . . . Madam / Of nothing / When . . . sleepe / Like . . . open Q1).

25–6   From Deuteronomy 28.15, 23.

CARIOLA
    Like to your picture in the gallery,
    A deal of life in show but none in practice;
    Or rather like some reverend monument
    Whose ruins are even pitied.
DUCHESS   Very proper:
    And Fortune seems only to have her eye-sight   35
    To behold my tragedy. How now,
    What noise is that?

[Enter SERVANT]

SERVANT   I am come to tell you
    Your brother hath intended you some sport:
    A great physician, when the Pope was sick
    Of a deep melancholy, presented him   40
    With several sorts of madmen, which wild object,
    Being full of change and sport, forced him to laugh,
    And so th'imposthume broke; the self-same cure
    The Duke intends on you.
DUCHESS   Let them come in.
SERVANT
    There's a mad lawyer, and a secular priest,   45
    A doctor that hath forfeited his wits
    By jealousy, an astrologian
    That in his works said such a day o'th'month
    Should be the day of doom, and failing oft,
    Ran mad; an English tailor crazed i'th'brain   50
    With the study of new fashion, a gentleman usher
    Quite beside himself with care to keep in mind
    The number of his lady's salutations,
    Or how do you, she employed him in each morning;
    A farmer too, an excellent knave in grain,   55
    Mad 'cause he was hind'red transportation;

31–2   From Sidney, *Arcadia* (*Works* I. 90).
33–4   Anticipating the setting of V.iii: to describe the ruins as 'reverend' implies that they
        remain sacred (though at the Dissolution, English monasteries were deconsecrated).
    43   *imposthume* abscess.
    45   *secular priest* One living in the world as contrasted with those who lived in monastic
        seclusion.
    55   *knave in grain* incorrigible rogue (and crooked dealer in corn or wheat).
    56   *transportation* export. Lucas notes a specific ruling of 1613 forbidding export of
        grain because of its high domestic price and fear of scarcity.

And let one broker that's mad loose to these,
You'd think the devil were among them!

DUCHESS

Sit, Cariola. [*To* SERVANT] – Let them loose when you please,
For I am chained to endure all your tyranny.   60

[*Enter* MADMEN]

Here, by a madman, this song is sung
to a dismal kind of music.

Oh let us howl some heavy note,
*   some deadly dogged howl,*
Sounding, as from the threat'ning throat
*   of beasts and fatal fowl.*
As ravens, screech-owls, bulls, and bears,   65
*   we'll bill and bawl our parts,*
Till irksome noise have cloyed your ears
*   and corrosived your hearts.*
At last whenas our choir wants breath,
*   our bodies being blest,*   70
We'll sing like swans to welcome death,
*   and die in love and rest.*

1 MADMAN

Doomsday not come yet? I'll draw it nearer by a perspective, or
make a glass that shall set all the world on fire upon an instant.
I cannot sleep, my pillow is stuffed with a litter of porcupines.   75

2 MADMAN

Hell is a mere glass-house, where the devils are continually
blowing up women's souls on hollow irons, and the fire never
goes out.

57   *broker* dealer, retailer.
60   s.d. The servant describes eight Madmen and Q1 assigns eight to dance, but allots
     the song only to one and speeches to four. Only the doctor is characterised
     consistently, and the text leaves open the choice, in performance, of the number of
     madmen and the way they are dressed.
60   s.d. 2 *song* The music, probably by Robert Johnson, has survived in several mss, and
     is in Brown and NCW.
66   *bill* Probably a nonce-word referring to the birds, meaning 'to utter through the bill
     or beak'; alternative readings such as *bell* (bellow) or *bawl* are appropriate to animals
     not birds.
73   *perspective* telescope, magnifying glass.
76   *glass-house* There was a glass factory in Blackfriars, and Webster refers to blown
     glass, shaped like a pregnant woman's belly, at II.ii.6–10.

3 MADMAN

I will lie with every woman in my parish the tenth night: I will
tithe them over like hay-cocks.   80

4 MADMAN

Shall my pothecary out-go me, because I am a cuckold? I have
found out his roguery: he makes allum of his wife's urine, and
sells it to Puritans that have sore throats with over-straining.

1 MADMAN

I have skill in heraldry.

2 MADMAN

Hast?   85

1 MADMAN

You do give for your crest a woodcock's head, with the brains
picked out on't: you are a very ancient gentleman.

3 MADMAN

Greek is turned Turk, we are only to be saved by the Helvetian
translation.

1 MADMAN

Come on sir, I will lay the law to you.   90

2 MADMAN

O, rather lay a corrosive, the law will eat to the bone.

3 MADMAN

He that drinks but to satisfy nature is damned.

4 MADMAN

If I had my glass here, I would show a sight should make all the
women here call me mad doctor.

1 MADMAN

What's he, a rope-maker?   95

2 MADMAN

No, no, no, a snuffling knave, that while he shows the tombs
will have his hand in a wench's placket.

---

86   *woodcock's* This bird was proverbially stupid and easy to catch.
87   *picked out* removed (and playing on the sense 'embroidered', associated with the idea
      of the heraldic crest).
88   *turned Turk* become an infidel (i.e. the Greek text of the Bible has been used to
      promote false religion).
88–9 The third Madman is apparently a Puritan, and Puritans were a frequent object of
      satire in the theatre of Webster's day: the Helvetian translation of the Bible – the
      Geneva Bible – of 1560, by Coverdale, Knox, and others, was strongly Calvinist in
      tone. It was condemned by King James I in 1603 as 'partial' and 'seditious'.
90   *lay the law* (1) expound the law (2) apply the law as a medicine, make a legal charge.
96   *snuffling* Probably alluding to the nasal whine affected by Puritans.
97   *placket* slit at the top of a skirt.

3 MADMAN

Woe to the caroche that brought home my wife from the masque at three o'clock in the morning, it had a large feather-bed in it.   100

4 MADMAN

I have pared the devil's nails forty times, roasted them in raven's eggs, and cured agues with them.

3 MADMAN

Get me three hundred milch bats, to make possets to procure sleep.

4 MADMAN

All the college may throw their caps at me, I have made a soap   105
boiler costive. It was my masterpiece.

Here the dance consisting of eight madmen,
with music answerable thereunto, after which

BOSOLA, *like an old man, enters*

DUCHESS

Is he mad too?

SERVANT   Pray question him: I'll leave you.

                         [*Exeunt* SERVANT *and* MADMEN]

BOSOLA

I am come to make thy tomb.

DUCHESS   Ha, my tomb?

Thou speak'st as if I lay upon my death bed
Gasping for breath: do'st thou perceive me sick?   110

BOSOLA

Yes, and the more dangerously since thy sickness is insensible.

DUCHESS

Thou art not mad sure; dost know me?

BOSOLA

Yes.

---

103   *possets* drinks of hot milk curdled by spiced wine or ale.
105   *throw their caps at me* concede my superiority.
105–6   *soap boiler costive* Diarrhoea was an occupational hazard in making soap; *costive* = constipated.
106   s.d. A parodic inversion of the form and values of the climactic dance in a marriage masque (where harmony, unity and order were symbolically expressed).
106   s.d. 3 *old man* Conventionally symbolic of Time and Death.
111   *insensible* Montaigne, *Essayes*, p. 397: 'And onely because we perceive not to be sicke, makes our recoverie to be more difficult'.

DUCHESS

Who am I?

BOSOLA

Thou art a box of worm-seed, at best, but a salvatory of green   115
mummy. What's this flesh? A little cruded milk, fantastical puff
paste: our bodies are weaker than those paper prisons boys use
to keep flies in – more contemptible, since ours is to preserve
earth worms. Didst thou ever see a lark in a cage? Such is the
soul in the body: this world is like her little turf of grass, and   120
the heaven o'er our heads like her looking-glass, only gives us a
miserable knowledge of the small compass of our prison.

DUCHESS

Am not I thy Duchess?

BOSOLA

Thou art some great woman sure, for riot begins to sit on thy
forehead, clad in grey hairs, twenty years sooner than on a   125
merry milkmaid's. Thou sleep'st worse than if a mouse should
be forced to take up her lodging in a cat's ear; a little infant that
breeds its teeth, should it lie with thee, would cry out as if thou
wert the more unquiet bed-fellow.

DUCHESS

I am Duchess of Malfi still.   130

BOSOLA

That makes thy sleeps so broken:
'Glories, like glow worms, afar off shine bright,
But looked to near, have neither heat nor light'.

DUCHESS

Thou art very plain.

---

115   *worm-seed* dried flower-heads of the plant were used as a remedy for intestinal
worms: and, alluding to the proverbial association of worms with corpses, there is
word-play on *seed* = germ, origin.
       salvatory ointment box.

115–16 *green mummy* medicine from mummified corpses; it was also believed that fresh
corpses could yield a medicinal balsam: this may explain *green*, although the colour
and its association with mouldy bones has a Websterian gruesomeness all its own.

116   *cruded* curded. Compare Donne, *Second Anniversary*, 165 (alluding to Job 10.10).

117   It was proverbial that 'the body is the prison of the soul' (Tilley B497). Webster may
also be recalling Shakespeare, *King Lear*, V.iii.8–9, where Lear, reunited with his
beloved daughter but captured, cries 'Come let's away to prison: / We two alone will
sing like birds i' th' cage'.

124   *riot* wantonness.

132–3 From *The White Devil*, V.i.40–41.

BOSOLA

My trade is to flatter the dead, not the living.   135
I am a tomb-maker.

DUCHESS

And thou com'st to make my tomb?

BOSOLA

Yes.

DUCHESS

Let me be a little merry. Of what stuff wilt thou make it?

BOSOLA

Nay, resolve me first, of what fashion?   140

DUCHESS

Why, do we grow fantastical in our death-bed, do we affect
fashion in the grave?

BOSOLA

Most ambitiously: princes' images on their tombs do not lie as
they were wont, seeming to pray up to heaven, but with their
hands under their cheeks as if they died of the toothache. They   145
are not carved with their eyes fixed upon the stars, but as their
minds were wholly bent upon the world the self-same way they
seem to turn their faces.

DUCHESS

Let me know fully therefore the effect
Of this thy dismal preparation,   150
This talk fit for a charnel.

BOSOLA   Now I shall.

        [*Enter* EXECUTIONERS *with*] *a* [*shrouded*] *coffin,*
                        cords and a bell

Here is a present from your princely brothers,
And may it arrive welcome, for it brings
Last benefit, last sorrow.

DUCHESS   Let me see it,
I have so much obedience in my blood   155
I wish it in their veins, to do them good.

BOSOLA

This is your last presence chamber.   [*Reveals the coffin*]

141–8   prose ed. (*Q1 lines ending* -bed / graue / tombes / pray / cheekes / carued / their /
         world / faces).
  152   s.d. The coffin is concealed under a pall or cloth.

CARIOLA
   Oh my sweet lady.
DUCHESS   Peace, it affrights not me.
BOSOLA
   I am the common bell-man,
   That usually is sent to condemned persons   160
   The night before they suffer.
DUCHESS   Even now thou said'st
   Thou wast a tomb-maker.
BOSOLA   'Twas to bring you
   By degrees to mortification. Listen:
        Hark now everything is still,
        The screech owl and the whistler shrill   165
        Call upon our dame, aloud,
        And bid her quickly don her shroud.
        Much you had of land and rent,
        Your length in clay's now competent;
        A long war disturbed your mind,   170
        Here your perfect peace is signed.
        Of what is't fools make such vain keeping?
        Sin their conception, their birth, weeping;
        Their life a general mist of error,
        Their death a hideous storm of terror.   175
        Strew your hair with powders sweet,
        Don clean linen, bathe your feet,
        And (the foul fiend more to check)

---

159   *bell-man* Here specified apparently to refer to a charity established by the Common
      Council of the Merchant Tailors guild (of which Webster's father was a member)
      which endowed a bell-man at Newgate Prison to make a speech outside the cell of
      condemned men the night before execution and another as they were taken to be
      hanged at Tyburn. Both speeches (accompanied by the tolling of a hand-bell) were
      to put them in mind of their mortality and urge them to save their souls. The bell
      is still extant, and on view in St Sepulchre's church – See Forker, pp. 21–4.
163   *mortification* The spiritual process ending in transcendence of one's earthly concerns
      and appetites (with a play on the sense 'the state of torpor and insensibility preceding
      death').
165   *whistler* Referred to as a fatal bird in Spenser, *Faerie Queene*, 2.12.36.
166   This invocation is the very opposite of that in an epithalamion or marriage-song,
      which conventionally bade such birds be silent on the wedding night.
169   *competent* appropriate, sufficient.
176   The Duchess is to prepare herself for burial in the same manner as a bride – in
      epithalamia brides are bid to strew their hair with sweet powders. A further irony is
      the echo of the Duchess' words at III.ii.58–9.

A crucifix let bless your neck.
'Tis now full tide 'tween night and day,   180
End your groan and come away.

CARIOLA

Hence villains, tyrants, murderers! Alas,
What will you do with my lady? Call for help!

DUCHESS

To whom? To our next neighbours? They are mad folks.

BOSOLA

Remove that noise.

[EXECUTIONERS *seize* CARIOLA]

DUCHESS   Farewell Cariola,   185
In my last will I have not much to give:
A many hungry guests have fed upon me.
Thine will be a poor reversion.

CARIOLA

I will die with her.

DUCHESS

I pray thee look thou giv'st my little boy   190
Some syrup for his cold, and let the girl
Say her prayers ere she sleep.

[EXECUTIONERS *force* CARIOLA *off*]
                    Now what you please:
What death?

BOSOLA   Strangling. Here are your executioners.

DUCHESS

I forgive them.
The apoplexy, catarrh, or cough o'th'lungs   195
Would do as much as they do.

BOSOLA

Doth not death fright you?

DUCHESS   Who would be afraid on't,
Knowing to meet such excellent company
In th'other world?

BOSOLA   Yet, methinks,
The manner of your death should much afflict you: 200
This cord should terrify you?

DUCHESS   Not a whit.
What would it pleasure me to have my throat cut

188   *reversion* bequest.
197–9   From Montaigne, *Essayes*, p. 75.

With diamonds, or to be smothered
With cassia, or to be shot to death with pearls?
I know death hath ten thousand several doors   205
For men to take their exits; and 'tis found
They go on such strange geometrical hinges,
You may open them both ways – any way, for heaven' sake,
So I were out of your whispering. Tell my brothers
That I perceive death, now I am well awake,   210
Best gift is they can give, or I can take.
I would fain put off my last woman's fault,
I'd not be tedious to you.

EXECUTIONER   We are ready.

DUCHESS

Dispose my breath how please you, but my body
Bestow upon my women: will you?

EXECUTIONER   Yes.   215

DUCHESS

Pull, and pull strongly, for your able strength
Must pull down heaven upon me –
Yet stay, heaven gates are not so highly arched
As princes' palaces: they that enter there
Must go upon their knees. [*Kneels*] Come violent death,   220
Serve for mandragora, to make me sleep.
Go tell my brothers when I am laid out,
They then may feed in quiet.

                                      They strangle her

BOSOLA

Where's the waiting woman?
Fetch her. Some other strangle the children.   225

                [EXECUTIONERS *fetch* CARIOLA,
                one goes to strangle the CHILDREN]

Look you, there sleeps your mistress.

CARIOLA   Oh you are damned
Perpetually for this! My turn is next,
Is't not so ordered?

BOSOLA   Yes, and I am glad
You are so well prepared for't.

CARIOLA   You are deceived, sir,
I am not prepared for't! I will not die!   230

205–6   *death . . . exits* From Seneca, and proverbial.
221   *mandragora* mandrake root, used as a narcotic (see II.v.1).

109

I will first come to my answer and know
How I have offended.

BOSOLA   Come, dispatch her.
You kept her counsel, now you shall keep ours.

CARIOLA
I will not die, I must not, I am contracted
To a young gentleman!

EXECUTIONER [*Shows noose*] Here's your wedding ring.   235

CARIOLA
Let me but speak with the Duke: I'll discover
Treason to his person.

BOSOLA   Delays: throttle her.

EXECUTIONER
She bites and scratches!

CARIOLA   If you kill me now
I am damned! I have not been at confession
This two years.

BOSOLA   When.

CARIOLA   I am quick with child.

BOSOLA   Why then,   240
Your credit's saved.

                                         [*They strangle her*]
                          Bear her into th'next room.
Let this lie still.

                          [*Exeunt* EXECUTIONERS *with* CARIOLA's *body*]

                          [*Enter* FERDINAND]

FERDINAND   Is she dead?

BOSOLA   She is what
You'd have her. But here begin your pity.

                          [*Draws the traverse and*] *shows the children strangled*
Alas, how have these offended?

FERDINAND   The death
Of young wolves is never to be pitied.   245

BOSOLA
Fix your eye here.

FERDINAND   Constantly.

BOSOLA   Do you not weep?

241   *credit* reputation.
242–6 ed. (Let . . . still / Is . . . dead / She is what / You'll'd . . . pitty / Alas . . . offended / The
       death / Of . . . pittied / Fix . . . here / Constantly / Do . . . weepe Q1).
243   s.d. A grim repetition of the s.d. at IV.i.54.

Other sins only speak; murder shrieks out.
The element of water moistens the earth,
But blood flies upwards and bedews the heavens.

FERDINAND

Cover her face. Mine eyes dazzle. She died young.   250

BOSOLA

I think not so; her infelicity
Seemed to have years too many.

FERDINAND

She and I were twins,
And should I die this instant I had lived
Her time to a minute.

BOSOLA   It seems she was born first: 255
You have bloodily approved the ancient truth
That kindred commonly do worse agree
Than remote strangers.

FERDINAND   Let me see her face again.
Why didst not thou pity her? What an excellent
Honest man might'st thou have been   260
If thou hadst borne her to some sanctuary
Or, bold in a good cause, opposed thyself
With thy advanced sword above thy head
Between her innocence and my revenge!
I bade thee, when I was distracted of my wits,   265
Go kill my dearest friend, and thou hast done't!
For let me but examine well the cause:
What was the meanness of her match to me?
Only, I must confess, I had a hope –
Had she continued widow – to have gained   270
An infinite mass of treasure by her death:

250   *Mine eyes dazzle* In IV.i The Duchess is associated with light, Ferdinand with
       darkness both spiritual and actual: he insists on visiting her in darkness, and later,
       in V.ii.62 speaks of his cruel sore eyes. See also lines 320–1 below; *dazzle* could also
       refer to the welling up of tears in Ferdinand's eyes – see Martin Wiggins, N&Q (Sep.
       1995) 372.
269–71 This constitutes an anomaly. At III.iii.66–7 it is asserted that the Duchess has a son
       by her first marriage. This corresponds to the sources but could be a relic of an early
       draft, a detail Webster accidentally failed to cancel, since if it is accepted it means that
       here Ferdinand – of all people – has somehow forgotten about his existence,
       although Webster makes Ferdinand the only person elsewhere in the play (III.iii.67)
       who refers to him: 'the Duke of Malfi, my young nephew'. Brown assumes Webster
       did intend to retain this son by the first marriage of the Duchess, and that here
       Ferdinand is deliberately trying to deceive Bosola or is making 'an instinctive'

And that was the main cause. Her marriage,
That drew a stream of gall quite through my heart.
For thee – as we observe in tragedies
That a good actor many times is cursed   275
For playing a villain's part – I hate thee for't;
And for my sake say, thou hast done much ill, well.

BOSOLA

Let me quicken your memory, for I perceive
You are falling into ingratitude: I challenge
The reward due to my service.

FERDINAND   I'll tell thee   280
What I'll give thee.

BOSOLA   Do.

FERDINAND   I'll give thee a pardon
For this murder.

BOSOLA   Ha?

FERDINAND   Yes: and 'tis
The largest bounty I can study to do thee.
By what authority did'st thou execute
This bloody sentence?

BOSOLA   By yours.

FERDINAND   Mine? Was I her judge?   285
Did any ceremonial form of law
Doom her to not-being? Did a complete jury
Deliver her conviction up i'th'court?
Where shalt thou find this judgement registered
Unless in hell? See, like a bloody fool   290
Th'hast forfeited thy life, and thou shalt die for't.

BOSOLA

The office of justice is perverted quite
When one thief hangs another. Who shall dare
To reveal this?

attempt to 'cover up' feelings of 'guilt'. Yet if it is assumed that Webster intends there
to be this son by the first marriage, then the first child the audience know about,
the first-born to the Duchess and Antonio, could inherit nothing except such
personal property as the Duchess is entitled to by her first marriage settlement and
/ or the dower after her first husband's death – scarcely an 'infinite mass of treasure'.
But the son born in Act II is presented in the closing moments of the play as a
symbol of hope for the future, so in performance it looks as if Webster did intend
to cancel the son by the first marriage.
274–91 A close parallel to Shakespeare, *Richard II*, V.vi.30–44, where Bolingbroke refuses to
reward the murderer of the King.

FERDINAND   Oh, I'll tell thee:
  The wolf shall find her grave and scrape it up,   295
  Not to devour the corpse but to discover
  The horrid murder.
BOSOLA   You, not I, shall quake for't.
FERDINAND
  Leave me.
BOSOLA   I will first receive my pension.
FERDINAND
  You are a villain.
BOSOLA   When your ingratitude
  Is judge, I am so.
FERDINAND   O horror,   300
  That not the fear of him which binds the devils
  Can prescribe man obedience.
  Never look upon me more.
BOSOLA   Why fare thee well.
  Your brother and yourself are worthy men,
  You have a pair of hearts are hollow graves,   305
  Rotten, and rotting others; and your vengeance,
  Like two chained bullets, still goes arm in arm.
  You may be brothers: for treason, like the plague,
  Doth take much in a blood. I stand like one
  That long hath ta'en a sweet and golden dream: 310
  I am angry with myself now that I wake.
FERDINAND
  Get thee into some unknown part o'th'world
  That I may never see thee.
BOSOLA   Let me know
  Wherefore I should be thus neglected. Sir,
  I served your tyranny, and rather strove   315
  To satisfy yourself than all the world;
  And though I loathed the evil yet I loved
  You, that did counsel it, and rather sought
  To appear a true servant than an honest man.

295–7   This superstition is referred to in *The White Devil*, V.iv.100–101.
307   *chained bullets* Cannon-balls linked by chain were used mainly in naval warfare to destroy masts and rigging but would also cut swathes through infantry in close order.
309   *take . . . blood* take hold in certain families.

FERDINAND

I'll go hunt the badger, by owl-light: 320
'Tis a deed of darkness.   *Exit*

BOSOLA

He's much distracted. Off, my painted honour;
While with vain hopes our faculties we tire,
We seem to sweat in ice, and freeze in fire;
What would I do, were this to do again?   325
I would not change my peace of conscience
For all the wealth of Europe –

                                    [DUCHESS *moves*]
                    She stirs! Here's life!
Return fair soul from darkness, and lead mine
Out of this sensible hell! She's warm, she breathes:
Upon thy pale lips I will melt my heart   330
To store them with fresh colour. [*Kisses her*] Who's there –
Some cordial drink! – Alas, I dare not call;
So pity would destroy pity. Her eye opes,
And heaven in it seems to ope, that late was shut,
To take me up to mercy.

DUCHESS   Antonio.   335

BOSOLA

Yes Madam he is living,
The dead bodies you saw were but feigned statues,
He's reconciled to your brothers, the Pope hath wrought
The atonement.

DUCHESS   Mercy.   *She dies*

BOSOLA

Oh, she's gone again: there the cords of life broke.   340
Oh sacred innocence that sweetly sleeps
On turtles' feathers, whilst a guilty conscience
Is a black register wherein is writ
All our good deeds and bad, a perspective

320   *owl-light* dusk.
327   s.d. Recalling the momentary revival of Desdemona in *Othello*, V.ii.117–25.
329   *sensible* perceptible, palpable.
332   *cordial* invigorating to the heart, reviving.
335   *mercy* ed. (merry Q1).
340   *cords of life* heart-strings.
344   *perspective* An optical device using mirrors, lenses etc. to produce special or fantastic effects. The effect of a guilty conscience is to rearrange past deeds, both good and bad, into a distorted prospect showing hell.

That shows us hell – that we cannot be suffered   345
To do good when we have a mind to it!
This is manly sorrow:
These tears, I am very certain, never grew
In my mother's milk. My estate is sunk
Below the degree of fear: where were   350
These penitent fountains while she was living?
Oh, they were frozen up. Here is a sight
As direful to my soul as is the sword
Unto a wretch hath slain his father.
Come, I'll bear thee hence   355
And execute thy last will; that's deliver
Thy body to the reverend dispose
Of some good women: that the cruel tyrant
Shall not deny me: then I'll post to Milan,
Where somewhat I will speedily enact   360
Worth my dejection.

Exit [*with the* DUCHESS' *body*]

354–5   ed. (*one line* Q1).
  361   *dejection* dismissal, humiliation.

115

ACT V, SCENE i

[*Enter* ANTONIO, DELIO]

ANTONIO
　What think you of my hope of reconcilement
　To the Aragonian brethren?

DELIO　　　　　　　　　　I misdoubt it;
　For though they have sent their letters of safe conduct
　For your repair to Milan, they appear
　But nets to entrap you. The Marquis of Pescara,　　　　　5
　Under whom you hold certain land in cheat,
　Much 'gainst his noble nature hath been moved
　To seize those lands, and some of his dependants
　Are at this instant making it their suit
　To be invested in your revenues.　　　　　　　　　　　10
　I cannot think they mean well to your life
　That do deprive you of your means of life –
　Your living.

ANTONIO　　　You are still an heretic
　To any safety I can shape myself.

[*Enter* PESCARA]

DELIO
　Here comes the Marquis: I will make myself　　　　　　15
　Petitioner for some part of your land,
　To know whether it is flying.

ANTONIO　　　　　　　　　I pray do.　　　　[*Withdraws*]

DELIO
　Sir, I have a suit to you.

PESCARA　　　　　To me?

DELIO　　　　　　　　　　An easy one:
　There is the citadel of Saint Bennet,
　With some demesnes, of late in the possession　　　　　20
　Of Antonio Bologna; please you bestow them on me?

　　0　s.d. ed. (ACTVS V. SCENA. I. / *Antonio, Delio, Pescara, Iulia.* Q1).
　　6　*in cheat* The property would revert to Pescara should Antonio be convicted of
　　　　treason or felony (as seems to be the case).
　11–12　Recalling *Merchant of Venice*, IV.i.376–7.
　　13　ed. (Your living / You . . . heretique Q1).

116

PESCARA

 You are my friend: But this is such a suit
 Nor fit for me to give nor you to take.

DELIO

 No sir?

       [*Enter* JULIA]

PESCARA

 I will give you ample reason for't   25
 Soon in private. Here's the Cardinal's mistress.

JULIA

 My lord, I am grown your poor petitioner,
 And should be an ill beggar, had I not
 A great man's letter, here, the Cardinal's, [*Presents letter*]
 To court you in my favour.

PESCARA   He entreats for you   30
 The citadel of Saint Bennet, that belonged
 To the banished Bologna.

JULIA   Yes.

PESCARA

 I could not have thought of a friend I could
 Rather pleasure with it: 'tis yours.

JULIA   Sir, I thank you,
 And he shall know how doubly I am engaged   35
 Both in your gift and speediness of giving,
 Which makes your grant the greater.   *Exit*

ANTONIO [*Aside*]   How they fortify
 Themselves with my ruin!

DELIO   Sir, I am
 Little bound to you.

PESCARA   Why?

DELIO

 Because you denied this suit to me, and gave't 40
 To such a creature.

PESCARA   Do you know what it was?
 It was Antonio's land: not forfeited
 By course of law but ravished from his throat
 By the Cardinal's entreaty: it were not fit
 I should bestow so main a piece of wrong   45
 Upon my friend, 'tis a gratification
 Only due to a strumpet, for it is injustice.

Shall I sprinkle the pure blood of innocents
To make those followers I call my friends
Look ruddier upon me? I am glad   50
This land, ta'en from the owner by such wrong,
Returns again unto so foul an use
As salary for his lust. Learn, good Delio,
To ask noble things of me, and you shall find
I'll be a noble giver.
DELIO   You instruct me well.   55
ANTONIO [*Aside*]
Why, here's a man, now, would fright impudence
From sauciest beggars.
PESCARA   Prince Ferdinand's come to Milan
Sick, as they give out, of an apoplexy;
But some say, 'tis a frenzy. I am going
To visit him.   *Exit*
ANTONIO [*Coming forward*] 'Tis a noble old fellow.   60
DELIO
What course do you mean to take, Antonio?
ANTONIO
This night I mean to venture all my fortune
Which is no more than a poor lingering life
To the Cardinal's worst of malice. I have got
Private access to his chamber and intend   65
To visit him about the mid of night
As once his brother did our noble Duchess.
It may be that the sudden apprehension
Of danger – for I'll go in mine own shape –
When he shall see it fraught with love and duty,   70
May draw the poison out of him, and work
A friendly reconcilement. If it fail,
Yet it shall rid me of this infamous calling:
For better fall once than be ever falling.
DELIO
I'll second you in all danger, and howe'er,   75
My life keeps rank with yours.
ANTONIO
You are still my loved and best friend.

                                              Exeunt

59   *frenzy* inflammation of the brain.
70   *fraught* ed. (fraight Q1).

118

[ACT V,] SCENE ii

[*Enter* PESCARA *and a* DOCTOR]

PESCARA
Now Doctor, may I visit your patient?
DOCTOR
    If 't please your lordship: but he's instantly
    To take the air here in the gallery,
    By my direction.
PESCARA   Pray thee, what's his disease?
DOCTOR
    A very pestilent disease, my lord,   5
    They call lycanthropia.
PESCARA   What's that?
    I need a dictionary to 't.
DOCTOR   I'll tell you:
    In those that are possessed with't there o'er-flows
    Such melancholy humour they imagine
    Themselves to be transformed into wolves: 10
    Steal forth to church-yards in the dead of night
    And dig dead bodies up: as two nights since
    One met the Duke 'bout midnight in a lane
    Behind St Mark's church, with the leg of a man
    Upon his shoulder; and he howled fearfully;   15
    Said he was a wolf, only the difference
    Was, a wolf's skin was hairy on the outside,
    His on the inside; bad them take their swords,

---

0   s.d. ed. (*SCENA. II. / Pescara, a Doctor, Ferdinand, Cardinall, Malateste, Bosola, Iulia. Q1*).

6   *lycanthropia* The name and the details in lines 8–19 come from Simon Goulart, *Admirable and Memorable Histories* (1607). Apparently lycanthropia was a fashionable subject for intellectuals: Donne owned a copy of Claude Prieur's *Dialogue de la lycanthropie, ou transformation d'hommes en loups, vulgairement dits loups-garous, et si telle se peut faire: auquel en discourant est traicté de la maniere de se contregarder des enchantements et sorcelleries, ensemble de plusiers abus et superstitions, lesquelles se commettent en ce temps*, Louvain, 1596 – see Jonathan Bate and Dora Thornton, *Shakespeare Staging the World*, 2012, p. 246.

14   *St Mark's church* Since no such church was located within the City of London, Marcus speculates that for audiences unfamiliar with Italy the name would probably have suggested the famous St Mark's in Venice rather than the less prominent one in Milan.

Rip up his flesh, and try. Straight I was sent for,
And having ministered to him, found his grace   20
Very well recovered.

PESCARA   I am glad on't.

DOCTOR
Yet not without some fear of a relapse:
If he grow to his fit again I'll go
A nearer way to work with him than ever
Paracelsus dreamed of: if they'll give me   25
Leave I'll buffet his madness out of him.
Stand aside, he comes.

[*Enter* CARDINAL, FERDINAND, MALATESTE,
and BOSOLA, *who stays apart*]

FERDINAND
Leave me.

MALATESTE
Why doth your lordship love this solitariness?

FERDINAND
Eagles commonly fly alone: they are crows, daws and starlings   30
that flock together. – Look, what's that follows me?

MALATESTE
Nothing, my lord.

FERDINAND
Yes.

MALATESTE
'Tis your shadow.

FERDINAND
Stay it, let it not haunt me.   35

MALATESTE
Impossible, if you move, and the sun shine.

FERDINAND
I will throttle it.

[*Throws himself on the ground*]

MALATESTE

25   *Paracelsus* Swiss physician and alchemist (1493–1541), famous as a serious scientist
     and physician while also the subject of many tall stories.
30–35 prose ed. (*Q1 lines ending* and / that / me / Lord / Yes / shadow / me).
31   *what's . . . me* There are proverbs, 'to be afraid of one's own shadow' and 'to fight with
     one's own shadow', but closer to the case of Ferdinand is an emblem for guilt in
     Whitney's *Choice of Emblemes* showing a man holding a sword fearing his own
     shadow. See R. E. R. Madeleine, *N&Q* (1982) 146.

Oh, my lord, you are angry with nothing.

FERDINAND

You are a fool. How is't possible I should catch my shadow
unless I fall upon't? When I go to hell, I mean to carry a bribe,   40
for look you, good gifts evermore make way for the worst
persons.

PESCARA

Rise, good my lord.

FERDINAND

I am studying the art of patience.

PESCARA

'Tis a noble virtue.   45

FERDINAND

To drive six snails before me, from this town to Moscow –
neither use goad nor whip to them, but let them take their own
time – the patient'st man i'th'world match me for an experi-
ment – and I'll crawl after like a sheep-biter.

CARDINAL

Force him up.   50

[They get FERDINAND *to his feet]*

FERDINAND

Use me well, you were best: what I have done, I have done, I'll
confess nothing.

DOCTOR

Now let me come to him. Are you mad, my lord? Are you out
of your princely wits?

FERDINAND

What's he?   55

PESCARA

Your doctor.

FERDINAND

Let me have his beard sawed off, and his eye-brows filed more
civil.

39–42   prose ed. (*Q1 lines ending* foole / shadow / Hell / you / persons).

46–9   prose ed. (*Q1 lines ending* towne / them / world / after / -biter).

49   *sheep-biter* dog that bites or worries sheep.

51–2   *what . . . nothing* Recalling *Othello,* V.ii.303–4.

51–4   prose ed. (*Q1 lines ending* best / nothing / mad / wits).

57–61   prose ed. (*Q1 lines ending* eye /civill / him / brought / you / -burning).

56–7   NCW suggest that if the part of Doctor is doubled by the boy-actor who earlier
played Cariola, the exaggerated false beard and eyebrows (conventional comedy
make-up) make appropriate heavy disguise for the actor.

DOCTOR

I must do mad tricks with him, for that's the only way on't. I
have brought your grace a salamander's skin, to keep you from   60
sun-burning.

FERDINAND

I have cruel sore eyes.

DOCTOR

The white of a cocatrice's egg is present remedy.

FERDINAND

Let it be a new laid one, you were best. – Hide me from him.
Physicians are like kings, they brook no contradiction.   65

DOCTOR

Now he begins to fear me, now let me alone with him.

CARDINAL

How now, put off your gown?

DOCTOR

Let me have some forty urinals filled with rose water: he and
I'll go pelt one another with them. Now he begins to fear me. –
Can you fetch a frisk, sir? – Let him go, let him go, upon my   70
peril.

[*They release* FERDINAND]

I find by his eye he stands in awe of me, I'll make him as tame
as a dormouse.

[FERDINAND *attacks the* DOCTOR]

FERDINAND

Can you fetch your frisks, sir? I will stamp him into a cullis, flay
off his skin to cover one of the anatomies this rogue hath set   75
i'th'cold yonder – in Barber Surgeons' hall! Hence! Hence! You
are all of you like beasts for sacrifice! There's nothing left of you
but tongue and belly, flattery and lechery!   [*Exit*]

---

60   *salamander's* The salamander was believed to live in fire.
63   *cockatrice's* the basilisk – see III.ii.87 n.
64–6 prose ed. (*Q1 lines ending* best / Kings / contradiction / me / him).
68–78 prose ed. (*Q1 lines ending* water / them / sir / perill / me / Dormouse / Cullice /
       Anotomies / hall / sacrifice / belly / leachery).
70   *fetch a frisk* cut a caper.
74   *cullis* meat broth.
75   *anatomies* skeletons.
76   *Barber Surgeons' hall* This chartered company was entitled to claim four corpses of
      executed felons per year for surgical dissection and experiment: it displayed
      specimen skeletons in the company's hall in Monkswell Street, Cripplegate.

PESCARA
　　Doctor, he did not fear you throughly.
DOCTOR
　　True, I was somewhat too forward.　　　　　　　　[*Exit*]　　80
BOSOLA [*Aside*]
　　Mercy upon me, what a fatal judgement
　　Hath fallen upon this Ferdinand.
PESCARA　　　　　　　　　　　　　　Knows your grace
　　What accident hath brought unto the Prince
　　This strange distraction?
CARDINAL [*Aside*]
　　I must feign somewhat. [*Aloud*] Thus they say it grew:　　85
　　You have heard it rumoured for these many years,
　　None of our family dies but there is seen
　　The shape of an old woman, which is given
　　By tradition to us, to have been murdered
　　By her nephews for her riches. Such a figure　　　　90
　　One night, as the Prince sat up late at's book,
　　Appeared to him: when crying out for help,
　　The gentlemen of's chamber found his grace
　　All on a cold sweat, altered much in face
　　And language; since which apparition　　　　　　95
　　He hath grown worse and worse, and I much fear
　　He cannot live.
BOSOLA [*To* CARDINAL]
　　Sir, I would speak with you.
PESCARA　　　　　　　　　　We'll leave your grace,
　　Wishing to the sick Prince, our noble lord,
　　All health of mind and body.
CARDINAL　　　　　　　　　You are most welcome.　　100
　　　　　　[*Exeunt all except* CARDINAL *and* BOSOLA]
　　Are you come? [*Aside*] So: this fellow must not know
　　By any means I had intelligence
　　In our Duchess' death, for though I counselled it,
　　The full of all th'engagement seemed to grow
　　From Ferdinand. [*To* BOSOLA] Now sir, how fares our sister?　　105
　　I do not think but sorrow makes her look
　　Like to an oft-dyed garment: she shall now
　　Taste comfort from me. Why do you look so wildly?
　　Oh, the fortune of your master here, the Prince,

104　　*engagement* employment (of Bosola).

123

Dejects you? But be you of happy comfort.   110
If you'll do one thing for me, I'll entreat
Though he had a cold tombstone o'er his bones
I'd make you what you would be.
BOSOLA   Any thing:
Give it me in a breath, and let me fly to't.
They that think long, small expedition win,   115
For musing much o'th'end, cannot begin.

[*Enter* JULIA]

JULIA
Sir, will you come in to supper?
CARDINAL   I am busy, leave me.
JULIA [*Aside*]
What an excellent shape hath that fellow!   *Exit*
CARDINAL
'Tis thus: Antonio lurks here in Milan,
Enquire him out, and kill him. While he lives   120
Our sister cannot marry, and I have thought
Of an excellent match for her. Do this, and style me
Thy advancement.
BOSOLA   But by what means shall I find him out?
CARDINAL
There is a gentleman called Delio
Here in the camp, that hath been long approved   125
His loyal friend: set eye upon that fellow,
Follow him to Mass; may be Antonio,
Although he do account religion
But a school-name, for fashion of the world,
May accompany him; or else go enquire out   130
Delio's confessor, and see if you can bribe
Him to reveal it. There are a thousand ways
A man might find to trace him, as to know
What fellows haunt the Jews for taking up
Great sums of money – for sure he's in want –   135

111 ' *one* ed. (on Q1).
125 *camp* Reminding the audience that the Cardinal has turned soldier (Brennan).
129 *school-name* From Sidney, *Arcadia* (*Works* II. 133): 'As for vertue, hee counted it but
     a schoole name' – a disparaging reference to the 'Schoolmen' of scholastic
     philosophy. Brown cites Bacon's view (*Advancement of Learning* I) that they
     produced 'cobwebs of learning, admirable for the fineness of thread and work, but
     of no substance or profit'.

Or else to go to th'picture makers and learn
Who brought her picture lately – some of these
Happily may take.
BOSOLA   Well, I'll not freeze i'th' business,
I would see that wretched thing Antonio
Above all sights i'th'world.
CARDINAL   Do, and be happy.   *Exit*   140
BOSOLA
This fellow doth breed basilisks in's eyes,
He's nothing else but murder; yet he seems
Not to have notice of the Duchess' death.
'Tis his cunning: I must follow his example,
There cannot be a surer way to trace   145
Than that of an old fox.

[*Enter* JULIA *pointing a pistol at him*]

JULIA   So, sir, you are well met.
BOSOLA
How now?
JULIA   Nay, the doors are fast enough.
Now sir, I will make you confess your treachery.
BOSOLA
Treachery?
JULIA   Yes, confess to me
Which of my women 'twas you hired, to put   150
Love-powder into my drink?
BOSOLA   Love powder?
JULIA
Yes, when I was at Malfi,
Why should I fall in love with such a face else?
I have already suffered for thee so much pain,
The only remedy to do me good   155
Is to kill my longing.
BOSOLA   Sure your pistol holds
Nothing but perfumes or kissing comfits; excellent lady,
You have a pretty way on't to discover

141   *basilisks* See III.ii.87 n.
146   s.d. Webster's stagecraft makes Julia's return parallel with Antonio's return, also
        carrying a pistol, at III.ii.140. Then Julia's wooing of Bosola is parallel (though clearly
        contrasting) to that of the Duchess' wooing of Antonio in Act I.
157   *kissing comfits* sweets perfumed to sweeten the breath.

Your longing: come, come, I'll disarm you,
And arm you thus.   [*Embracing her*]
            Yet this is wondrous strange.   160

JULIA

Compare thy form and my eyes together,
You'll find my love no such great miracle. Now you'll say
I am wanton; this nice modesty in ladies
Is but a troublesome familiar
That haunts them.   165

BOSOLA

Know you me. I am a blunt soldier.

JULIA   The better,
Sure. There wants fire, where there are no lively sparks
Of roughness.

BOSOLA   And I want compliment.

JULIA   Why, ignorance
In courtship cannot make you do amiss
If you have a heart to do well.

BOSOLA   You are very fair.   170

JULIA

Nay, if you lay beauty to my charge
I must plead unguilty.

BOSOLA   Your bright eyes
Carry a quiver of darts in them sharper
Than sun-beams.

JULIA   You will mar me with commendation,
Put yourself to the charge of courting me,   175
Whereas now I woo you.

BOSOLA [*Aside*]

I have it, I will work upon this creature. –
[*To* JULIA] Let us grow most amorously familiar.
If the great Cardinal now should see me thus,
Would he not count me a villain?   180

JULIA

No, he might count me a wanton,
Not lay a scruple of offence on you:
For if I see and steal a diamond,
The fault is not i'th'stone but in me the thief

167–8   *fire . . . roughness* From Sidney, *Arcadia* (*Works* I. 452–3).
168 –9   ed. (Of . . . roughnes / And . . . compliment / Why . . . amisse Q1).
168–70   *ignorance . . . well* From Sidney, *Arcadia* (*Works* I. 106).

That purloins it. I am sudden with you: 185
We that are great women of pleasure, use to cut off
These uncertain wishes and unquiet longings
And in an instant join the sweet delight
And the pretty excuse together. Had you been in th'street,
Under my chamber window, even there 190
I should have courted you.
BOSOLA   Oh, you are an excellent lady.
JULIA
Bid me do somewhat for you presently
To express I love you.
BOSOLA   I will; and if you love me,
Fail not to effect it.
The Cardinal is grown wondrous melancholy: 195
Demand the cause, let him not put you off
With feigned excuse; discover the main ground on't.
JULIA
Why would you know this?
BOSOLA   I have depended on him,
And I hear that he is fallen in some disgrace
With the Emperor. If he be, like the mice 200
That forsake falling houses, I would shift
To other dependence.
JULIA   You shall not need follow the wars,
I'll be your maintenance.
BOSOLA   And I your loyal servant;
But I cannot leave my calling.
JULIA   Not leave an
Ungrateful general, for the love of a sweet lady? 205
You are like some cannot sleep in feather-beds,
But must have blocks for their pillows.
BOSOLA   Will you do this?
JULIA
Cunningly.
BOSOLA   Tomorrow I'll expect th'intelligence.
JULIA
Tomorrow? Get you into my cabinet,

187–9   *wishes . . . excuse* From Sidney, *Arcadia* (*Works* I. 452).
   191   ed. (I . . . you / Oh . . . Lady Q1).
   193   ed. (To . . . you / I . . . me Q1).
194–5   ed. (Fail . . . mellancholly Q1).

You shall have it with you. Do not delay me,   210
No more than I do you. I am like one
That is condemned: I have my pardon promised,
But I would see it sealed. Go, get you in,
You shall see me wind my tongue about his heart
Like a skein of silk.   215

                                [*Exit* BOSOLA]

       [*Enter* CARDINAL *followed by* SERVANTS]

CARDINAL
   Where are you?
SERVANTS   Here.
CARDINAL   Let none upon your lives
   Have conference with the Prince Ferdinand
   Unless I know it.

                       [*Exeunt* SERVANTS]

   [*Aside*]   In this distraction
   He may reveal the murder.
   Yond's my lingering consumption: 220
   I am weary of her and by any means
   Would be quit off.
JULIA   How now, my lord,
   What ails you?
CARDINAL   Nothing.
JULIA   Oh, you are much altered.
   Come, I must be your secretary and remove
   This lead from off your bosom. What's the matter?   225
CARDINAL
   I may not tell you.
JULIA   Are you so far in love with sorrow
   You cannot part with part of it? Or think you
   I cannot love your grace when you are sad,
   As well as merry? Or do you suspect
   I, that have been a secret to your heart   230
   These many winters, cannot be the same
   Unto your tongue?
CARDINAL   Satisfy thy longing,
   The only way to make thee keep my counsel
   Is not to tell thee.

210–13   *delay . . . sealed* From Sidney, *Arcadia* (*Works* II. 31).

JULIA   Tell your echo this –
  Or flatterers, that like echoes still report   235
  What they hear, though most imperfect – and not me:
  For if that you be true unto yourself,
  I'll know.
CARDINAL   Will you rack me?
JULIA   No, judgement shall
  Draw it from you. It is an equal fault,
  To tell one's secrets unto all, or none.   240
CARDINAL
  The first argues folly.
JULIA   But the last tyranny.
CARDINAL
  Very well – why, imagine I have committed
  Some secret deed which I desire the world
  May never hear of.
JULIA   Therefore may not I know it?
  You have concealed for me as great a sin   245
  As adultery: sir, never was occasion
  For perfect trial of my constancy
  Till now: sir, I beseech you.
CARDINAL   You'll repent it.
JULIA   Never.
CARDINAL
  It hurries thee to ruin. I'll not tell thee,
  Be well advised, and think what danger 'tis   250
  To receive a prince's secrets: they that do
  Had need have their breasts hooped with adamant
  To contain them. I pray thee yet be satisfied,
  Examine thine own frailty; 'tis more easy
  To tie knots than unloose them: 'tis a secret   255
  That like a ling'ring poison may chance lie
  Spread in thy veins, and kill thee seven year hence.
JULIA
  Now you dally with me.
CARDINAL   No more: thou shalt know it.
  By my appointment the great Duchess of Malfi
  And two of her young children, four nights since   260
  Were strangled.
JULIA   Oh heaven! Sir, what have you done!

CARDINAL

How now, how settles this? Think you, your
Bosom will be a grave dark and obscure enough
For such a secret?

JULIA   You have undone yourself, sir.

CARDINAL

Why?

JULIA   It lies not in me to conceal it.   265

CARDINAL

No? Come, I will swear you to't upon this book.

JULIA

Most religiously.

CARDINAL   Kiss it.

                                    [*She kisses the book*]

Now you shall never utter it. Thy curiosity
Hath undone thee. Thou'rt poisoned with that book;
Because I knew thou couldst not keep my counsel,   270
I have bound thee to't by death.

                        [*Enter* BOSOLA]

BOSOLA

For pity sake, hold!

CARDINAL   Ha, Bosola!

JULIA   I forgive you
This equal piece of justice you have done,
For I betrayed your counsel to that fellow,
He overheard it: that was the cause I said   275
It lay not in me to conceal it.

BOSOLA   Oh foolish woman,
Couldst not thou have poisoned him?

JULIA   'Tis weakness
Too much to think what should have been done.
I go I know not whither.   [*She dies*]

CARDINAL

Wherefore com'st thou hither?   280

BOSOLA

That I might find a great man like yourself,

267   *religiously* If Julia kneels the spectators will recognise a visual parallel with the death
        of the Duchess; at the same time Julia dies with the conventional words of a dying
        sinner, contrasting to the firm faith of the Duchess.
271   *thee* ed. (the Q1).

Not out of his wits as the Lord Ferdinand,
To remember my service.

CARDINAL   I'll have thee hewed in pieces!

BOSOLA

Make not yourself such a promise of that life
Which is not yours to dispose of.   285

CARDINAL

Who placed thee here?

BOSOLA   Her lust, as she intended.

CARDINAL

Very well, now you know me for your fellow murderer.

BOSOLA

And wherefore should you lay fair marble colours
Upon your rotten purposes to me,
Unless you imitate some that do plot great treasons   290
And, when they have done, go hide themselves i'th'graves
Of those were actors in't?

CARDINAL   No more,
There is a fortune attends thee.

BOSOLA

Shall I go sue to Fortune any longer?
'Tis the fool's pilgrimage.   295

CARDINAL

I have honours in store for thee.

BOSOLA

There are a many ways that conduct to seeming
Honour, and some of them very dirty ones.

CARDINAL

Throw to the devil
Thy melancholy. The fire burns well,   300
What need we keep a stirring of it, and make
A greater smother? Thou wilt kill Antonio?

BOSOLA

Yes.

CARDINAL Take up that body.

BOSOLA   I think I shall
Shortly grow the common bier for church-yards.

288–9   A further metaphor from painting, the wording close to Sidney, *Arcadia*, (*Works* I. 260).

297–8   For the proverbial quality of this remark compare Francis Bacon's observation that the roads to riches are many and most of them foul.

CARDINAL

    I will allow thee some dozen of attendants   305
    To aid thee in the murder.

BOSOLA   Oh, by no means.

    Physicians that apply horse-leeches to any rank swelling, use
    to cut off their tails, that the blood may run through them the
    faster: let me have no train when I go to shed blood, lest it make
    me have a greater when I ride to the gallows.   310

CARDINAL

    Come to me after midnight to help to remove that body to her
    own lodging: I'll give out she died o'th'plague, 'twill breed the
    less enquiry after her death.

BOSOLA

    Where's Castruchio, her husband?

CARDINAL

    He's rode to Naples to take possession of Antonio's citadel.   315

BOSOLA

    Believe me, you have done a very happy turn.

CARDINAL

    Fail not to come. There is the master-key
    Of our lodgings, and by that you may conceive
    What trust I plant in you.   *Exit*

BOSOLA   You shall find me ready.

    Oh poor Antonio, though nothing be so needful   320
    To thy estate as pity, yet I find
    Nothing so dangerous. I must look to my footing;
    In such slippery ice-pavements men had need
    To be frost-nailed well, they may break their necks else.
    The precedent's here afore me: how this man   325
    Bears up in blood, seems fearless! Why, 'tis well:
    Security some men call the suburbs of hell,
    Only a dead wall between. Well, good Antonio,
    I'll seek thee out, and all my care shall be

307–13   prose ed. (*Q1 lines ending* swelling / them / blood / Gallowes / body / Plague / death).

317   *master-key* A parallel to Bosola's procuring for Ferdinand the key to the Duchess' bedchamber in III.i.80.

325   *precedent's* ed. (President's Q1).

326   *Bears up in blood* Probably deriving from hunting terms – 'keeps his courage' (so Lucas); Brown suggests 'persists in shedding blood'.

327   *Security* If of the spiritual kind, security was believed dangerous because implying undue confidence in salvation; if carnal, dangerous because implying undue concern for this life and indifference to the next world.

328   *dead* continuous.

To put thee into safety from the reach 330
Of these most cruel biters that have got
Some of thy blood already. It may be
I'll join with thee in a most just revenge:
The weakest arm is strong enough that strikes
With the sword of justice. – Still methinks the Duchess 335
Haunts me! There there, 'tis nothing but my melancholy.
O penitence, let me truly taste thy cup,
That throws men down, only to raise them up.

Exit [*with* JULIA's *body*]

[ACT V,] SCENE iii

[*Enter* ANTONIO *and* DELIO]

DELIO

Yond's the Cardinal's window. This fortification
Grew from the ruins of an ancient abbey,
And to yond side o'th'river lies a wall,
Piece of a cloister, which in my opinion
Gives the best echo that you ever heard, 5

338 s.d. A visual parallel to Bosola's previous exit with the Duchess' body in IV.ii.

0 s.d. ed. (SCENA III. / *Antonio, Delio, Eccho,* (*from the Dutchesse Graue.*) Q1).
0 s.d. The s.d. for Echo seems to be directed to readers; it makes no reference to any visual special effect, and Delio does say (45) that Antonio only imagines seeing the Duchess' face; but Antonio's description (44–5), as Brown notes, corresponds to a s.d. in *The Second Maiden's Tragedy* (acted by the King's Men in 1611):
    On a sodayne in a kinde of Noyse like a Wynde, the dores clattering, the Toombstone flies open, and a great light appeares in the midst of the Toombe; His Lady as went owt, standing iust before hym all in white, Stuck with Iewells and a great crucifex on her brest.
    Webster perhaps saw this piece of machinery among the properties of the King's Men.
1 *Yond* In the original performance Delio presumably would point to the tiring-house backing the stage (with its openings at the upper level) to indicate the exterior of the Cardinal's house. Antonio's reference to *here in this open court* presumably indicates the main stage where they stand; other features – the wall and *piece of a cloister* – could be left wholly to the spectator's imagination. The echoes would be spoken off-stage by the actor who played the Duchess. If an actual tomb-property was used, it was probably placed in the central opening in the tiring-house.

So hollow and so dismal and withal
So plain in the distinction of our words
That many have supposed it is a spirit
That answers.

ANTONIO   I do love these ancient ruins.
We never tread upon them but we set   10
Our foot upon some reverend history,
And questionless, here in this open court
Which now lies naked to the injuries
Of stormy weather, some men lie interred
Loved the church so well, and gave so largely to't,   15
They thought it should have canopied their bones
Till doomsday; but all things have their end:
Churches and cities, which have diseases like to men,
Must have like death that we have.

ECHO   *Like death that we have.*

DELIO
Now the echo hath caught you.

ANTONIO   It groaned, methought, and gave   20
A very deadly accent.

ECHO   *Deadly accent.*

DELIO
I told you 'twas a pretty one: you may make it
A huntsman, or a falconer, a musician,
Or a thing of sorrow.

ECHO   *A thing of sorrow.*

ANTONIO
Ay sure, that suits it best.

ECHO   *That suits it best.*   25

ANTONIO
'Tis very like my wife's voice.

ECHO   *Ay, wife's voice.*

DELIO
Come: let's walk farther from't.
I would not have you go to th'Cardinal's tonight:
Do not.

ECHO   *Do not.*

9–11   From Montaigne, *Essayes*, pp. 596–7.
19   Echo's lines are italicised in Q1.
27   *let's* ed. (let's us Q1).
28   *go* Q1b (too Q1a).

DELIO
    Wisdom doth not more moderate wasting sorrow   30
    Than time: take time for't, be mindful of thy safety.
ECHO
Be mindful of thy safety.
ANTONIO   Necessity compels me.
    Make scrutiny throughout the passes
    Of your own life; you'll find it impossible
    To fly your fate.
[ECHO]   *O fly your fate.*   35
DELIO
    Hark: the dead stones seem to have pity on you
    And give you good counsel.
ANTONIO
    Echo, I will not talk with thee,
    For thou art a dead thing.
ECHO   *Thou art a dead thing.*
ANTONIO
    My Duchess is asleep now,   40
    And her little ones, I hope sweetly: oh heaven
    Shall I never see her more?
ECHO   *Never see her more.*
ANTONIO
    I marked not one repetition of the echo
    But that: and on the sudden a clear light
    Presented me a face folded in sorrow.   45
DELIO
    Your fancy, merely.
ANTONIO   Come, I'll be out of this ague;
    For to live thus is not indeed to live:
    It is a mockery and abuse of life.
    I will not henceforth save myself by halves,
    Lose all, or nothing.
DELIO   Your own virtue save you!   50
    I'll fetch your eldest son and second you:
    It may be that the sight of his own blood
    Spread in so sweet a figure, may beget

33   *passes* events.
35   s.p. ed. (not in Q1).
42   *never see her more* Antonio echoes his own words at III.v.81.
44–5   See n. to line 1 above.

The more compassion.

[ANTONIO]   How ever, fare you well.

Though in our miseries Fortune have a part,   55

Yet in our noble suff'rings she hath none.

Contempt of pain – that we may call our own.

Exeunt

[ACT V,] SCENE iv

[*Enter* CARDINAL, PESCARA, MALATESTE,
RODERIGO, *and* GRISOLAN]

CARDINAL

You shall not watch tonight by the sick Prince,

His grace is very well recovered.

MALATESTE

Good my lord, suffer us.

CARDINAL   Oh, by no means.

The noise, and change of object in his eye,

Doth more distract him. I pray, all to bed,   5

And though you hear him in his violent fit,

Do not rise, I entreat you.

PESCARA   So sir, we shall not.

CARDINAL

Nay, I must have your promise

Upon your honours, for I was enjoined to't

By himself; and he seemed to urge it sensibly.   10

---

54   s.p. ed. (not in Q1) follows Q1 where the page ends at 'compassion' and the
     catchword is 'How' with no sign that a s.p. has been omitted. Nevertheless I consider
     a compositor's error is likely: the change of speaker would allow this scene to end
     focused on Antonio, which seems dramatically right.

0   s.d. ed. (SCENA. IIII. / *Cardinall, Pescara, Malateste, Rodorigo, Grisolan, Bosola,
     Ferdinand, Antonio, Seruant. Q1*).

1   *tonight* The time is close to midnight (see line 23). Since performances at the open
     amphitheatre playhouses took place in daylight, and the Blackfriars theatre
     auditorium was candle-lit not darkened, actors carried torches, candles or (as here)
     lanterns, as conventional indication of night.

PESCARA
    Let our honours bind this trifle.
CARDINAL
    Nor any of your followers.
MALATESTE   Neither.
CARDINAL
    It may be, to make trial of your promise
    When he's asleep, myself will rise and feign
    Some of his mad tricks, and cry out for help,   15
    And feign myself in danger.
MALATESTE   If your throat were cutting
    I'd not come at you, now I have protested against it.
CARDINAL
    Why, I thank you.   *[Walks apart]*
GRISOLAN   'Twas a foul storm tonight.
RODERIGO
    The Lord Ferdinand's chamber shook like an osier.
MALATESTE
    'Twas nothing but pure kindness in the devil,   20
    To rock his own child.
                      Exeunt [all but CARDINAL]
CARDINAL
    The reason why I would not suffer these
    About my brother, is, because at midnight
    I may with better privacy convey
    Julia's body to her own lodging.   25
    Oh, my conscience!
    I would pray now, but the devil takes away my heart
    For having any confidence in prayer.

             [Enter BOSOLA *behind]*

    About this hour I appointed Bosola
    To fetch the body: when he hath served my turn,   30
    He dies.   *Exit*
BOSOLA
    Ha? 'Twas the Cardinal's voice: I heard him name
    Bosola, and my death. – Listen, I hear one's footing.

   10   *sensibly* with strong feeling.
   11   *our* ed. (out Q1).
   16   *cutting* being cut.
25–6   ed. (*one line* Q1).

[*Enter* FERDINAND]

FERDINAND
Strangling is a very quiet death.
BOSOLA [*Aside*]
Nay then, I see I must stand upon my guard.   35
FERDINAND
What say to that? Whisper, softly: do you agree to't?
So. It must be done i'th'dark – the Cardinal
Would not for a thousand pounds the Doctor should see it.

Exit

BOSOLA
My death is plotted. Here's the consequence of murder.
'We value not desert, nor Christian breath,   40
When we know black deeds must be cured with death'.

[*Enter* ANTONIO *and* SERVANT]

SERVANT
Here stay sir, and be confident, I pray.
I'll fetch you a dark lantern.   *Exit*
ANTONIO
Could I take him at his prayers,
There were hope of pardon.
BOSOLA   Fall right my sword: 45
I'll not give thee so much leisure as to pray.

[BOSOLA *wounds* ANTONIO]

ANTONIO
Oh, I am gone! Thou hast ended a long suit
In a minute.
BOSOLA   What art thou?
ANTONIO   A most wretched thing,
That only have thy benefit in death,
To appear myself.

[*Enter* SERVANT *with a lantern*]

SERVANT   Where are you sir?   50

34   *quiet* ed. (quiein Q1).
44–5   Bosola, unable to identify the speaker in the darkness, mistakes Antonio for a cut-
        throat and misinterprets his words as meaning 'If I could kill Bosola at his prayers
        the Cardinal would give me a pardon'.
50   NCW suggest that the servant brings a light (a theatrical signal that the action must
        be imagined as in darkness) so enabling Antonio and Bosola to recognise each other.

ANTONIO
    Very near my home. – Bosola?
SERVANT   Oh misfortune!
BOSOLA
    Smother thy pity, thou art dead else. – Antonio?
    The man I would have saved 'bove mine own life?
    We are merely the stars' tennis balls, struck and banded
    Which way please them. Oh good Antonio,   55
    I'll whisper one thing in thy dying ear
    Shall make thy heart break quickly: thy fair Duchess
    And two sweet children –
ANTONIO   Their very names
    Kindle a little life in me –
BOSOLA   Are murdered!
ANTONIO
    Some men have wished to die   60
    At the hearing of sad tidings. I am glad
    That I shall do't in sadness. I would not now
    Wish my wounds balmed, nor healed, for I have no use
    To put my life to: in all our quest of greatness,
    Like wanton boys whose pastime is their care,   65
    We follow after bubbles blown in the air.
    Pleasure of life, what is't? Only the good hours
    Of an ague; merely a preparative to rest,
    To endure vexation. I do not ask
    The process of my death: only commend me   70
    To Delio.
BOSOLA   Break heart.
ANTONIO
    And let my son fly the courts of princes.   [*Dies*]
BOSOLA
    Thou seem'st to have loved Antonio?
SERVANT   I brought him hither
    To have reconciled him to the Cardinal.

54–5   A Renaissance tag, but the phrasing is very close to Sidney, *Arcadia* (*Works* II. 177),
        where men 'are but like tenisballs, tossed by the racket of the hyer powers'; see also
        Sir William Alexander, *The Alexandraean Tragedy*, 5.1 in *The Monarchicke Tragedies*,
        1607. 'I thinke the world is but a tennis-court, / Where men are tossde by fortune as
        her balls'.
  59   A contrast to the comforting words Bosola speaks to the dying Duchess at IV.ii.336–9.
        Delivered abruptly, the line can provoke laughter in an audience.
  62   *sadness* earnest.

BOSOLA

I do not ask thee that: 75
Take him up, if thou tender thine own life,
And bear him where the Lady Julia
Was wont to lodge. Oh, my fate moves swift.
I have this Cardinal in the forge already,
Now I'll bring him to th'hammer. Oh direful misprision,   80
I will not imitate things glorious
No more than base; I'll be mine own example.
[*To* SERVANT] On, on, and look thou represent, for silence,
The thing thou bear'st.
                              Exeunt [BOSOLA *and* SERVANT *with* ANTONIO's
body]

[ACT V,] SCENE v

[*Enter* CARDINAL, *with a book*]

CARDINAL

I am puzzled in a question about hell:
He says, in hell there's one material fire,
And yet it shall not burn all men alike.
Lay him by. How tedious is a guilty conscience!
When I look into the fish-ponds in my garden   5
Methinks I see a thing armed with a rake
That seems to strike at me.

[*Enter* BOSOLA *and* SERVANT *with* ANTONIO's *body*]

Now! Art thou come? Thou look'st ghastly:
There sits in thy face some great determination,

---

80   *misprision* mistake.
84   s.d. Webster's stagecraft makes a point by repetition: Bosola has already carried out
       the dead bodies of the Duchess (IV.ii) and Julia (V.ii).

0   s.d. ed. (SCENA. V. / *Cardinall* (*with a Booke*) Bosola, Pescara, Malateste, Rodorigo,
       Ferdinand, Delio, Seruant with Antonio's body. Q1).
0   s.d. *with a book* A conventional stage sign of melancholy (as in *Hamlet*, 2.2.167).
4   *tedious* If the Cardinal uses the word in the sense 'tiresome' he is being cynical, if in
       the sense 'painful', he is seriously troubled. Either is possible.

Mixed with some fear.

BOSOLA   Thus it lightens into action: 10
I am come to kill thee.

CARDINAL   Ha? Help! Our guard!

BOSOLA
Thou art deceived, they are out of thy howling.

CARDINAL
Hold: and I will faithfully divide
Revenues with thee.

BOSOLA   Thy prayers and proffers
Are both unseasonable.

CARDINAL   Raise the watch!   15
We are betrayed!

BOSOLA   I have confined your flight:
I'll suffer your retreat to Julia's chamber,
But no further.

CARDINAL   Help! We are betrayed!

[*Enter, above,* PESCARA, MALATESTE, RODERIGO,
GRISOLAN]

MALATESTE   Listen.

CARDINAL
My dukedom, for rescue!

RODERIGO   Fie upon his counterfeiting.

MALATESTE
Why, 'tis not the Cardinal.

RODERIGO   Yes, yes, 'tis he: 20
But I'll see him hanged ere I'll go down to him.

CARDINAL
Here's a plot upon me! I am assaulted! I am lost
Unless some rescue!

GRISOLAN   He doth this pretty well,
But it will not serve to laugh me out of mine honour.

CARDINAL
The sword's at my throat!

RODERIGO   You would not bawl so loud then.   25

MALATESTE

10–12   ed. (Mixed ... feare / Thus ... Action / I ... thee / Hah ... Guard / Thou ... deceiu'd
/ They ... howling Q1).

14–16   ed. (Revenewes ... thee / Thy ... proffers / Are ... vnseasonable / Raise ... betraid
/ I ... flight Q1).

19   *My ... rescue* Recalling *Richard III*, V.iv.1–7.

Come, come, let's go to bed, he told us thus much aforehand.

PESCARA
He wished you should not come at him, but believe't,
The accent of the voice sounds not in jest.
I'll down to him, howsoever, and with engines
Force ope the doors.   [*Exit above*]

RODERIGO   Let's follow him aloof,   30
And note how the Cardinal will laugh at him.

                                        [*Exeunt above*]

BOSOLA
There's for you first –

                              He kills the SERVANT

'Cause you shall not unbarricade the door
To let in rescue.

CARDINAL
What cause hast thou to pursue my life?

BOSOLA   Look there.   35

CARDINAL
Antonio?

BOSOLA   Slain by my hand unwittingly.
Pray, and be sudden. When thou kill'dst thy sister
Thou took'st from Justice her most equal balance
And left her nought but her sword.

CARDINAL   Oh mercy!

BOSOLA
Now it seems thy greatness was only outward,   40
For thou fall'st faster of thyself than calamity
Can drive thee. I'll not waste longer time – there!

                    [BOSOLA *wounds the* CARDINAL]

CARDINAL
Thou hast hurt me.

BOSOLA   Again!

                              [*Wounds him again*]

CARDINAL   Shall I die like a leveret
Without any resistance? Help! Help! Help!
I am slain!   45

                    [*Enter* FERDINAND]

32–5   ed. (There's ... doore / To ... rescew / What ... life / Looke there Q1).

FERDINAND

Th'alarum? Give me a fresh horse!
Rally the vaunt-guard, or the day is lost!
Yield! Yield! I give you the honour of arms,
Shake my sword over you. Will you yield?

CARDINAL

Help me! I am your brother.

FERDINAND   The devil?   50
My brother fight upon the adverse party?
There flies your ransom!

He wounds the CARDINAL, *and (in the scuffle)*
gives BOSOLA *his death wound*

CARDINAL

Oh justice!
I suffer now for what hath former been:
'Sorrow is held the eldest child of sin'.   55

FERDINAND

Now you're brave fellows: Caesar's fortune was harder than Pompey's, Caesar died in the arms of prosperity, Pompey at the feet of disgrace: you both died in the field. The pain's nothing: pain, many times, is taken away with the apprehension of greater – as the tooth-ache with the sight of a barber that comes   60 to pull it out. There's philosophy for you.

BOSOLA

Now my revenge is perfect: sink, thou main cause
Of my undoing!

He kills FERDINAND

            The last part of my life
Hath done me best service.

FERDINAND

Give me some wet hay, I am broken winded.   65

46   Ferdinand (to grotesque and absurd effect) imagines he is on the battlefield (see *Richard III*, V.iii.177, where Richard starts up out of a nightmare crying 'Give me another horse!'). For those spectators who recognise the quotation the absurdity will be doubled – Ferdinand believing himself to be a king in a famous Shakespeare play and speaking lines from it. In the original production the effect would have been further enhanced for those spectators who recognised that the actor playing Ferdinand (Burbage), had himself played the Shakespearean role of Richard III.

51   This scuffle is evidently to be as clumsy and confused as possible, the very opposite of high tragic style.

56–61   prose ed. (*Q1 lines ending* fellowes / *Pompey's* / prosperity / field / with / sight / you).

65   *wet hay* Treatment for broken-winded horses recommended in Gervase Markham, *Markham's Maister-peece*, 1610, p. 101 (so Lucas).

I do account this world but a dog-kennel:
I will vault credit and affect high pleasures
Beyond death.

BOSOLA   He seems to come to himself
Now he's so near the bottom.

FERDINAND
My sister! Oh my sister, there's the cause on't!   70
'Whether we fall by ambition, blood, or lust,
Like diamonds we are cut with our own dust'.   [*Dies*]

CARDINAL
Thou hast thy payment too.

BOSOLA
Yes, I hold my weary soul in my teeth,
'Tis ready to part from me. I do glory   75
That thou, which stood'st like a huge pyramid
Begun upon a large and ample base,
Shalt end in a little point, a kind of nothing.

[*Enter* PESCARA, MALATESTE, RODERIGO, GRISOLAN]

PESCARA
How now, my lord?

MALATESTE   Oh sad disaster.

RODERIGO   How comes this?

BOSOLA
Revenge for the Duchess of Malfi, murdered   80
By th'Aragonian brethren; for Antonio,
Slain by this hand; for lustful Julia,
Poisoned by this man; and lastly, for myself,
That was an actor in the main of all,
Much 'gainst mine own good nature, yet i'th'end   85
Neglected.

PESCARA   How now, my lord?

CARDINAL   Look to my brother.
He gave us these large wounds as we were struggling
Here i'th'rushes. And now, I pray, let me
Be laid by, and never thought of.

68–9   ed. (Beyond death. / He . . . bottom. Q1).
74   *soul in my teeth* From Montaigne, *Essayes*, II. p. 430.
82   this ed. (his Q1).
88   *rushes* Customarily strewn on the Elizabethan stage.

PESCARA
How fatally, it seems, he did withstand   90
His own rescue!
MALATESTE   Thou wretched thing of blood,
How came Antonio by his death?
BOSOLA
In a mist: I know not how;
Such a mistake as I have often seen
In a play. Oh I am gone.   95
We are only like dead walls, or vaulted graves,
That ruined, yields no echo. Fare you well.
It may be pain but no harm to me, to die
In so good a quarrel. Oh this gloomy world!
In what a shadow, or deep pit of darkness,   100
Doth womanish and fearful mankind live!
Let worthy minds ne'er stagger in distrust
To suffer death or shame for what is just.
Mine is another voyage.   [Dies]
PESCARA
The noble Delio, as I came to th'palace,   105
Told me of Antonio's being here, and showed me
A pretty gentleman, his son and heir.

[Enter DELIO with ANTONIO's SON]

MALATESTE
Oh sir, you come too late.
DELIO   I heard so, and
Was armed for't ere I came. Let us make noble use
Of this great ruin; and join all our force   110
To establish this young hopeful gentleman
In's mother's right. These wretched eminent things

96   *dead* continuous, unbroken.
100–1 *shadow . . . live* From Sidney, *Arcadia* (*Works* II 177): 'such a shadowe, or rather pit
       of darkenes, the wormish mankinde lives'.
112   *mother's right* See IV.ii.269–71 n. There is a reference at III.iii.66–7 to the Duchess
       having had a son by her first marriage: a child who, though a minor, is Duke of
       Malfi. Yet the Duchess never refers to any such son by her first marriage nor, of
       course, do the audience see one, whereas Webster stresses the Duchess' exceptional
       concern for her children born of the marriage to Antonio, and their presence in
       several scenes of the play is very significant. Delio here presents Antonio's son, as sole
       survivor, in public as a symbol of political hope, as successor to his mother. His
       horoscope – see II.iii.57–65 – may give cause for anxiety, but Webster's treatment of
       it in Act II is ambivalent. Given the importance of this final theatrical and narrative

Leave no more fame behind 'em than should one
Fall in a frost and leave his print in snow:
As soon as the sun shines, it ever melts,   115
Both form, and matter. I have ever thought
Nature doth nothing so great, for great men,
As when she's pleased to make them lords of truth:
'Integrity of life is fame's best friend,
Which nobly, beyond death, shall crown the end'.   120

Exeunt

FINIS

emphasis on the surviving son it seems likely that Webster changed his mind during composition of the play and decided to diverge from his sources, making the Duchess childless until she married Antonio, but he failed to correct the text accordingly. Otherwise the *mother's right* would refer, lamely, not to the dukedom, since this has already passed to her son by her first marriage (she has only been administering it during his minority); it would refer only to such property as the Duchess retained personally after her marriages. This boy would then represent the (fragile) survival of his parents' spiritual values and their love.

117–18   From Sidney, *Arcadia* (*Works* I. 190).
119–20   Alluding to Horace, *Odes* I xxii. Horace's phrase 'integer vitae' was itself a commonplace, so probably the implied irony would be appreciated only by the more understanding members of Webster's audience. Yet this quotation is bedevilled by the ironic sting in the quotation's tail, for Horace later in the Ode also says that not even a wolf would attack a man possessed of integrity of life. The Duchess certainly was attacked by the wolf-man Ferdinand, and she does resort to public deceptions: but against that an audience can balance her unwavering constancy to a private faith.

APPENDIX

Collation of BM 644.f.72 Q1 lineation

(* also in text commentary)

I.i

4	ed. (How ... court / I ... it Q1)*
29	ed. (I ... still / So / I ... you Q1)
128–30	prose ed. (Nor ... saies / Too ... her / Too ... wrinckle Q1)*
165	ed. (All ... fashion / Twins / In qualitie Q1)
170	ed. (Rewards ... heare-say / Then ... him Q1)
173	ed. (To ... him / Most true Q1)
198	ed. (And ... her / Fye Antonia Q1)
204–5	ed. (Some ... hence / I shall / Sister ... you / To me Sir Q1)*
207	ed. (One ... Gallies / Yes ... him Q1)
209	ed. (The ... horse / Your ... him Q1)
210	ed. (Commends ... him / Call ... heither Q1)
211	are now Q4 (now Q1)
213	ed. (At ... Leagues / Sir ... shall / You ... *Millaine* / I am Q1)*
220	ed. (Had ... fitter / You ... him Q1)
222	ed. (He ... you / I ... you Q1)
230	ed. (He ... wrongfully / For that Q1)
234	ed. (Fastens ... roote / Yet ... heed Q1)
237	ed. (And ... you / There's gold / So Q1)
239–40	ed. (*one line* Q1)*
247	ed. (I ... againe / No sir Q1)
249–50	ed. (I ... not / It ... me / One ... familiars / Familiar ... that Q1)*
252	ed. (An intelligencer / Such ... thing Q1)
254	ed. (At ... by't / Take ... Diuels Q1)
261	ed. (Have ... out / Noe / 'Tis ... thankes Q1)
268	ed. (That ... complementall / Be ... selfe Q1)
273	ed. (May ... dormouse / As ... some Q1)
284	ed. (Must ... director / You ... Widowe Q1)
288–90	ed. (Sway ... blood / Marry ... luxurious / Will ... twice / O fie / Their ... spotted / Then ... sheepe / Diamonds ... value Q1)*
292–3	ed. (Whores ... precious / Will ... me / I'll ...marry / So ... say Q1)
296	ed. (And ... together / Now ... me Q1)
307	ed. (Will ... light / You ... your selfe Q1)
309	ed. (Under ... night / Think't ... voyage Q1)
314–15	ed. (To ... celibrated / The ... night / Is ... prison / And ... ioyes Q1)*
317	ed. (Which ...mischief / Fare ... well Q1)
320	ed. (It ... off / You ... sister Q1)
327	ed. (Hath ... in't / Fye Sir / Nay Q1)
340	ed. (More ... fame / Both ... safe Q1)
344	ed. (Keep ... children / Thy protestation Q1)
345	ed. (Is ... come / He ... you / Good ... soule Q1)

147

352–4   ed. (Take ... ready / Yes / What ... say / That ... -what / Oh ... remember Q1)*
358–61 ed. (So ... Excellence / Beauteous... sake / You ... you / I'le ... the / Particulars ...
           expence Q1)*
365   ed. (What's ... me / Where / In Heaven Q1)
371   ed. (That ... distruction / Oh ... better Q1)
378–9   ed. (Give ... all / All / Yes ... selfe / In ... sheete / In ... cople Q1)*
382   ed. (To ... againe / What ... marriage Q1)
385   ed. (There's ... in't / How ... it Q1)
387   ed. (Would ... thus / Pray ... it Q1)
393   ed. (Like ... Starling / Fye ... this Q1)
403   ed. (Is ... circle / Remoove him / How Q1)
405   ed. (May ... fit / What ... you / Sir Q1)
418   ed. (To ... them / So ... broake Q1)
430   ed. (And ... her / Now ... it Q1)
451   ed. (Of ... name / I ... loue Q1)
458   ed. (But ... Brothers / Do ... them Q1)
462   ed. (Scatter ... tempest / These ... mine Q1
464   ed. (Would ... flattery / Kneele / Hah Q1)
471   ed. (Be ... motion / Quickning ... make Q1)
479   ed. (Our ... wishes / How ... faster Q1)
482   ed. (I ... blinde / What's ... this Q1)

II.i

3–11   prose ed. (*Q1 lines ending* already/ largely / a / sentence / againe / in / if / scape)*
14–20   prose ed. (*Q1 lines ending* quarrel / seldome / valiant / me / fellow / it / you / you /
           -caps)*
23–8   prose ed. (*Q1 lines ending* -physicke / neere / rutts / progresse / pockes / leuell /
           Nutmeg-grater / hedge-hog)*
30–1   prose ed. (*Q1 lines ending* old / againe / plastique)*
33–41   prose ed. (*Q1 lines ending* witch-craft / spittle / face / feete / fasting / very / his /
           his / leafe / -selues)*
59–60   prose ed. (Your ... you / To ...aches Q1)*
69   ed. (The ... yeelds / And ... married Q1)
70   ed. (You ... me / Let ... euer Q1)
74–90   prose ed. (*Q1 lines ending* contemplation / fellow / tettor / simplicity / happy /
           from the / honest / in-side / so / world / continue / leave it / any/ you / reach /
           horses / suit / me / gallop / tyre)*
93–103   prose ed. (*Q1 lines ending* ascendant / your / lineally / himselfe / in / water /
           brought / persons / them / makes / -pig / spoile / goodly / Cannon)*
113   ed. (So ... mother / I ... much Q1)
115–17   ed. (I ... it / In ... Presence / Yes Q1)
123   ed. (Put ... first / You ... me Q1)
126–8   ed. (I ... Grace / For me sir / Apricocks Madam / O ... they / I ... yeare / Good ...
           rises Q1)*
131–2   ed. (We ... moneth / Will ... them Q1)
135–6   ed. (Why / I ... Gardner Q1)
138–40   ed. (Did ... -doung / Oh ... iest / You ... one / Indeed Madam / I ... fruit / Sir ...
           loath Q1)*
142   ed. (They ... restorative / 'Tis ... pretty / Art ... grafting Q1)
152   ed. (If ... sicke / How ... Madame Q1)

154–5   ed. (How ... me / Nay ... already / Oh ... sweat / I ... sorry Q1)
157   ed. (I ... vndone / Lights ... lights Q1)
160   ed. (No ... remoue / Have ... prepar'd Q1)
167–8   ed. (For ... close / Fye ... Physitians / Will ... her / For ... pretend Q1)

II.ii

1–3   prose ed. (*Q1 lines ending* teatchiues / apparant / now)
26   ed. (Shut ...gates / Why ... danger Q1)
28–30   ed. (All ...Court / I ... instantly / Who ...–gate / *Forobosco* / Let ...presently Q1)
34–5   ed. (There ... Switzer / In ... Bed-chamber Q1)
51   ed. (Are ... shut / Yes / 'Tis ... pleasure Q1)
61   ed. (How ... Dutchesse / She's expos'd Q1)
66   ed. (My ... seruice / Doe ... me Q1)
68   ed. (Somewhat ... danger / Beleeve it Q1)
71   ed. (Your ... you / Blessed comfort Q1)

II.iiii

13   ed. (I ... friend. / *Bosola* Q1)
15–18   ed. (A ... now / From whence / From ... lodging / Not ... you / I ... dream'd / Let's ... it / No ... 'twas / But ... winde / Very likely Q1)*
20–2   ed. (You ... wildly / I ... figure / For ... Iewells / Ah ... question / Doe ... radicall / What's ... you Q1)*
25   ed. (Makes ... –walker / In ... you Q1)
29   ed. (You ... Courtier / This ... me Q1)
31–4   ed. (Pray ...poysond / Poysond ... figge / For ... imputation / Traitors ... confident / Till ... too Q1)*
36   ed. (More ... selfe / You ... steward Q1)
42–4   ed. (You ... sir / No sir / Copy ... to't / My ... count Q1)*
47–8   ed. (Are ... order Q1)*

II.iv

3   ed. (Without ... husband / Why ... him Q1)
5–6   ed. (Heare ... devotion / Thou ... one / I ... him / You ... me Q1)
8   ed. (Find ... inconstant / Doe ... selfe Q1)
10   ed. (Out ... guilt / How ... Lord Q1)
13–14   ed. (Did ... them / Sooth ... woemen / A man ... male-able Q1)
15   ed. (Ere he ... fixed / So ... Lord Q1)
20   ed. (This ... Lord / Why ... weepe Q1)
26–7   ed. (You ... cuckould / I'll ... home / To ... husband / You ... Lady Q1)
39   ed. (And ... physicke / Who's that Q1)
41   ed. (Lightning ... to't / Madam ... Gentleman Q1)
43–4   ed. (Let ... with-draw / He sayes / Your ... *Rome* Q1)
47–8   ed. (I ... you / Sir ... wel-come / Do ... here / Sure ... experience Q1)*
50   ed. (Do ... Ladies / Very well Q1)
52   ed. (For ... him / I ... *Rome* Q1)
56–7   ed. (His ... sore / Your laughter / Is ... pitty / Lady ... whether Q1)
59   ed. (From ... husband / No ... allowance Q1)
63   ed. (Try ... on't / A ... it Q1)

67	ed. (This . . . by - / Your . . . come Q1)
72	ed. (As . . . be / With . . . you Q1)
76	ed. (And . . . answere / Very fine Q1)

II.v

1–2	ed. (I . . . man-drake / Say you / And . . . with't / What's . . . progedy Q1)
4	ed. (Growne . . . Strumpet / Speak lower / Lower Q1)*
11–12	ed. (Then . . . Seruice / Is't possible / Can . . . certaine / Rubarbe . . . rubarbe Q1)
16–17	ed. (To . . . out / Why . . . selfe / So . . . Tempest / Would . . . one Q1)
21	ed. (As . . . honors / Shall . . . blood Q1)
23	ed. (Be . . . attaincted / Apply . . . physicke Q1)
29	ed. (I'll . . . Bastard / What . . . do Q1)
31	ed. (When . . . peeces / Curs'd creature Q1)
33	ed. (So . . . left-side / Foolish men Q1)
36–7	ed. (Apt . . . it / Thus / Ignorance . . . honour Q1)*
38	ed. (It . . . it / Methinkes . . . laughing Q1)
41	ed. (To . . . sinne / With whom Q1)
46	ed. (You . . . reason / Goe . . . Mistris Q1)
48–50	ed. (But . . . blood / How . . . rage / Which . . . ayre Q1)
54–5	ed. (To . . . imperfection / Have . . . you / My palsey / Yes . . . angry Q1)
66	ed. (By her / Are . . . mad / I . . . bodies Q1)
73	ed. (The . . . backe / I'll . . . you / Nay . . . done Q1)

III.i

16	ed. (Your . . . hasten / 'Pray . . . me Q1)
18	ed. (Of . . . *Cardinall* / I . . . hath Q1)
20	ed. (Doth . . . dangerously / Pray why Q1)
24	ed. (Till . . . vp / What . . . people Q1)
26	ed. (She . . . Strumpet / And . . . heades Q1)
37–8	ed. (They . . . off / The . . . *Ferdinand* / Is . . . bed / I'll . . . bed Q1)
40–1	ed. (A . . . you / For . . . is't / The . . . *Malateste* / Fie . . . him Q1)
48	ed. (Touching . . . honour / Let . . . to't Q1)
55–6	ed. (In . . . innocency / O . . . comfort / This . . . purg'd / Her . . . on Q1)
58	ed. (How . . . intelligence / Sir vncertainly Q1)
60	ed. (By . . . Starres / Why some Q1)
64	ed. (Us'd . . . Duchesse / Sorcery . . . purpose Q1)
66	ed. (She . . . acknowledge / Can . . . way Q1)
81–2	ed. (Into . . . -chamber / I haue / As . . . wish / What . . . doe / Can . . . ghesse / No Q1)
86–90	ed. (And . . . -sands / I . . . not / Thinke so / What . . . pray / That . . . are / Your . . . grosly / Flatter . . . selfe / Give . . . thee Q1)*

III.ii

3	ed. (Indeed . . . one / Very good Q1)
7	ed. (I . . . here / Must . . . Misse-rule Q1)
9	ed. (To . . . me / We'll . . . together Q1)
12	ed. (She'll . . . you / See . . . of Q1)
15	ed. (Sir . . . question / I . . . *Cariola* Q1)
17	ed. (Do . . . early / Labouring men Q1)

19   ed. (Are . . . ended / I'll . . . mouth Q1)
22   ed. (When . . . *Cariola* / Never . . . Lord Q1)
44   ed. (What is't / I . . . Ladies Q1)
67–8 Q4; (*one line* Q1)
70   ed. (I . . . Prince / Die . . . quickle Q1); s.d. Q1b (not in Q1a)*
72   ed. (Is . . . thee / 'Pray . . . me Q1)
74   ed. (And . . . thing / Sir / Doe . . . speak Q1)
82   ed. (I . . . married / So Q1)
86–8 ed. (Will . . . Husband / Yes . . . I / Could. . . Basilisque / Sure . . . hither / By . . . consideracy / The . . . Wolfe Q1)*
109   ed. (Lest . . . him / Why . . . marry Q1)
111   ed. (Any . . . cvstome / Thou . . . vndone Q1)
114   ed. (About . . . heart / Mine . . . for't / Thine . . . heart Q1)
116   ed. (Fill'd . . . wild-fire / You . . . this Q1)
119   ed. (Is safe / Dost . . . is Q1)
136   ed. (I . . . more / Why . . . I Q1)
139   ed. (And . . . beautie / So . . . Virgins Q1)
141   ed. (You . . . apparition / Yes . . . are Q1)
143   ed. (This . . . that / Pray . . . when Q1)
145   ed. (Mine innocence / That . . . entrance Q1)
149–51 ed. (He . . . me / And . . . wish / You . . . selfe / His Action / Seem'd . . . much /This . . . to't Q1)
154   ed. (How . . . Earthquakes / I stand Q1)
156   ed. (To . . . vp / 'Tis *Bosola* / Away Q1)
161   ed. (Hath . . . Rome / So late Q1)
163   ed. (You . . . vndone / Indeed . . . it Q1)
170   ed. (Strange . . . cunning / And hereupon Q1)
172   ed. (Against . . . Officers / I shall Q1)
202   ed. (As . . . downe / We . . . confiscate Q1)
204–5 ed. (All . . . haue / I . . . fit / All . . . so / So . . . Passe Q1)
211   ed. (I . . . opinions / Of . . . Antonio Q1)
212–23 prose ed. (*Q1 lines ending* gaping / Iew / sake / money / came / hearing / woman / full / goe / him / Chaine)*
263–5 ed. (I . . . Politisians / Rotten . . .hart-string Q1)
269–70 ed. (That . . . fall /Was . . . vertue Q1)
271   ed. (Oh . . . Musicke / Say you Q1)
277   ed. (I . . . him / Fortunate Lady Q1)
302   ed. (To *Ancona* / So / Whether . . . dayes Q1)
303   ed. (I . . . thee / Let . . . thinke Q1)
309–10 ed. (Your . . . you /Sir . . . direction / Shall . . . hand / In . . . opinion Q1)

III.iiii

1   ed. (Must . . . then? / The Emperour Q1)
5–9   ed. (And . . . *Lanoy* / He . . . honour / Of . . . Prisoner / The same / Here's . . . Fortification / At *Naples* / This . . . perceive / Hath . . . employment / No . . . Lord Q1)
11   ed. (A . . . Lord / He's . . . souldier Q1)
20   ed. (Battalles . . . modell / Then . . . booke Q1)
23   ed. (That's . . . skarfe / Yes . . . protests Q1)
26   ed. (To . . .prisoner / He . . . afraid Q1)
39   ed. (About . . . for't / What's . . . *Bosola* Q1)

40–45   prose ed. (*Q1 lines ending* scholler / in / was / - ach / the / this / man)*
49–51   prose ed (*Q1 lines ending* oppression / ones / storme)*
52   ed. (The . . . laughes / Like . . . Cannon Q1)
56–60   ed. (In . . . charmes / Doth . . . hood / To . . . tempest / That . . . and / Beauty . . . leaprosie Q1)*
64   ed. (To . . . banish'd / You . . . *Loretto* Q1)
68   ed. (With's . . . honesty / I will / *Antonio* Q1)

III.iv

2   ed. (Yet . . . many / The . . . *Arragon* Q1)
6   ed. (A . . . Ceremony / No . . . come Q1)
26   ed. (Beares . . . cruell / They . . . banish'd Q1)
33   ed. (But . . . justice / Sure . . . none Q1)
36   ed. (Of . . . finger / 'Twas . . . ring Q1)
38   ed. (To . . . reuenge / Alasse *Antonio* Q1)

III.v

1–3   ed. (Banish'd *Ancona* / Yes . . . powre / Lightens . . . breath / Is . . . traine / Shrunke . . . remainder / These . . . men Q1)*
6   ed. (Now . . . gon / They . . . wisely Q1)
9   ed. (Their Patients / Right . . . world Q1)
12   ed. (I . . . night / What was't Q1)
15   ed. (Were . . . Pearles / My interpretation Q1)
17   ed. (Doe . . . teares / The . . . field Q1)
21   ed. (You . . . ore-ta'ne / From . . . brother Q1)
36   ed. (And . . . too / What . . . beleeve Q1)
46–7   ed. (And . . . you / Thus . . . come / And . . . this / My . . . dispers'd Q1)
54   ed. (You . . . from's / I . . . Ambush Q1)
58   ed. (In . . . bottom / You . . . safely Q1)
63   ed. (To . . . order / I . . . best Q1)
69   ed (I . . . thus / Oh . . . comfort Q1)
77–8   ed. (And . . . right / But . . . –sticke / Doe . . . weepe Q1)
92   ed. (Make . . . vs / O . . . welcome Q1)
104   ed. (To none / Whether then / To your Pallace Q1)
107–8   ed. (Your . . . pitie / Pitie . . . aliue Q1)*
110   ed. (To . . . eaten / These . . . children / Yes / Can . . . prattle / No Q1)*
112–13   ed. (Curses . . . language / Fye Madam / Forget . . . -fellow / Were . . . man Q1)
115   ed. (One . . . birth / Say . . . meane Q1)*

IV.i

2   ed. (In her imprisonment / Nobly . . . her Q1)
12   ed. (With . . . disdaine / 'Tis . . . restraint Q1)
15   ed. (Those . . . from / Curse . . . her Q1)
18   ed. (All . . . Grace / I . . . none Q1)
28–9   ed. (He . . . you / At . . . pleasure / Take . . . come Q1)*
30–31   ed. (Where . . . you / Here sir /This . . . well / I . . . pardon / You . . . it Q1)*
37   ed. (Makes . . . equall / Doe . . . this Q1)
39   ed. (Shall . . for't / It . . . well Q1)
44   ed. (You gave / I . . . it Q1)

50	ed. (Whether . . . you / You . . . cold Q1)
52	ed. (Hah . . . horrible / Let . . . enough Q1)
65	ed. (For . . . mercy / What's that Q1)
67	ed. (And . . . death / Come . . . live Q1)
72–4	ed. (Of . . . wife / O . . . remember / You . . . Christian / The . . . fasting / I'll . . . death / Leave . . . sorrow Q1)
77	ed. (May . . . –lid / Good . . . fellow Q1)
85	ed. (Now . . . you / Thou . . . then Q1)
89	ed. (What . . . you / One . . . life Q1)
93	ed. (I'll . . . curse / O fye / I . . . Starres / Oh fearfull Q1)
97–9	ed. (Looke . . . still / Oh . . . goe / Plagues . . . families Q1)
100	ed. (Consume them / Fie Lady / Let . . . tyrants Q1)
103	ed. (Church-men . . . them / O vncharitable Q1)
105–6	ed. (To . . . bleed Q1)
112–13	ed. (For . . . Bodies / Why . . . this / To . . . despaire / 'Faith . . . here Q1)
117	ed. (With . . . bookes / Damne . . . hers Q1)
129	ed. (Must . . . againe / Yes Never / You must Q1)
133	ed. (The . . . comfort / Very likely Q1)

IV.ii

1	ed. (What . . . that / 'Tis . . . consort Q1)
9	ed. (O . . . mellancholly / Thou . . . deceiu'd Q1)
15–17	ed. (What . . . Madam / Of nothing / When . . . sleepe / Like . . . open Q1)*
37	ed. (What . . . that / I . . . you Q1)
44	ed. (The . . . you / Let . . . in Q1)
107–8	ed. (Is . . . to / 'Pray . . . you / I . . . tombe / Hah . . . tombe Q1)
136–9	ed. (I . . . tombe-maker / And . . . tombe / Yes / Let . . . merry Q1)
141–8	prose ed. (Q1 *lines ending* -bed / graue / tombes / pray / cheekes / carued / their / world / faces)*
151	ed. (This . . . charnell / Now I shall Q1)
154	ed. (Last . . . sorrow / Let . . . it Q1)
158	ed. (O . . . Lady / Peace . . . me Q1)
161–2	ed. (The . . . suffer / Even . . . said'st / Thou . . . tombe-maker / 'Twas . . . you Q1)
185	ed. (Remoove . . . noyse / Farewell *Cariola* Q1)
193	ed. (What . . . death / Strangling . . . executioners Q1)
197	ed. (Doth . . . you / Who . . . on't Q1)
199	ed. (In . . . world / Yet . . . thinkes Q1)
213	ed. (I'l'd . . . you / We . . . ready Q1)
226	ed. (Look . . . mistris / Oh . . . damn'd Q1)
229	ed. (You . . . for't / You . . . Sir Q1)
232	ed. (How . . . offended / Come . . . her Q1)
235	ed. (To . . . Gentle-man / Here's . . . Ring Q1)
237–8	ed. (Treason . . . person / Delays . . . throttle-her / She . . . scratches / If . . . now Q1)
240	ed. (This two yeeres / When / I . . . child / Why then Q1)
242–6	ed. (Let . . . still / Is . . . dead / She is what / You'll'd . . . pitty / Alas . . . offended / The death / Of . . . pittied / Fix . . . here / Constantly / Do . . . weepe Q1)*
255	ed. (Her . . . Mynute / It . . . first Q1)
258	ed. (Then . . . strangers / Let . . . againe Q1)
280–2	ed. (The . . . service / I'll . . . thee / Doe / I'll . . . pardon / For . . . murther / Hah / Yes . . . 'tis Q1)

285   ed. (This . . . yours / Mine . . . Judge Q1)
297–9   ed. (The . . . murther / You . . . for't / Leave me / I . . . Pention / You . . . villaine / When . . . Ingratitude Q1)
335–6   ed. (To . . . mercy / *Antonio* / Yes . . . liuing Q1)
339   ed. (The atonement / Mercy Q1)
354–5   ed. (*one line in* Q1)

V.i

13   ed. (Your living / You . . . heretique Q1)*
30   ed. (To . . . fauour / He . . . you Q1)
32–4   ed. (To . . .*Bologna* / Yes / I . . . could / Rather . . . yours / Sir . . . you Q1)
37–9   ed. (Which . . . greater / How . . . fortefie / Themselves . . . ruine / Sir . . . am / Little . . . you / Why Q1)
41   ed. (To . . . creature / Doe . . . was Q1)
57   ed. (From . . . Beggers / Prince . . . *Millaine* Q1)
60   ed. (To . . . him / 'Tis . . . fellow Q1)

V.ii

4   ed. (By . . . direction / 'Pray . . . disease Q1)
30–35   prose ed. (*Q1 lines ending* and / that / me / Lord / Yes / shadow / me)*
39–42   prose ed. (*Q1 lines ending* foole / shadow / Hell / you / persons)*
46–9   prose ed. (*Q1 lines ending* towne / them / world / after / -biter)*
51–4   prose ed. (*Q1 lines ending* best / nothing / mad / wits)*
57–61   prose ed. (*Q1 lines ending* eye /civill / him / brought / you / -burning)*
64–6   prose ed. (*Q1 lines ending* best / Kings / contradiction / me / him)*
68–78   prose ed. (*Q1 lines ending* water / them / sir / perill / me / Dormouse / Cullice / Anotomies / hall / sacrifice / belly / leachery)*
82   ed. (Hath . . . *Ferdinand* / Knows . . . grace Q1)
97   ed. (He . . . Live / Sir . . . you / We'll . . . grace Q1)
100   ed. (All . . . body / You . . . welcome Q1)
113   ed. (I'll'd . . . be / Any thing Q1)
117   ed. (Sir . . . Supper / I . . . me Q1)
123   ed. (Thy . . . advancement / But . . . out Q1)
138   ed. (Happily . . . take / Well . . . businesse Q1)
140   ed. (Above . . . world / Do . . . happy Q1)
146–7   ed. (Then . . . Fox / So . . . met / How now / Nay . . . enough Q1)
149   ed. (Treachery / Yes . . . me Q1)
151   ed. (Love- . . . drinke / Love powder Q1)
156   ed. (Is . . . longing / Sure . . . holds Q1)
162   ed. (You'll . . . say Q1)
166   ed. (Know . . . soldier / The better Q1)
168–9   ed. (Of roughnes / And . . . compliment / Why . . . amisse Q1)*
170   ed. (If . . . well / You . . . faire Q1)
172   ed. (I . . . unguilty / Your . . . eyes Q1)
174   ed. (Then Sun-beames / You . . . commendation Q1)
191   ed. (I . . . you / Oh . . . Lady Q1)*
193   ed. (To . . . you / I . . . me Q1)*
194–5   ed. (Fail . . . mellancholly Q1)*
198   ed. (Why . . . this / I . . . him Q1)

202–4	ed. (To ... dependance / You ... warres / I'll ... maintenance / And ... seruant / But ... calling / Not ... an Q1)
207–8	ed. (But ... pillowes / Will ... this / Cunningly / To morrow ... intelligence Q1)
216	ed. (Where ... you / Here / Let ... liues Q1)
222–3	ed. (Would ... off / How ... Lord / What ... you / Nothing / O ... alterd Q1)
226	ed. (I ... you / Are ... sorrow Q1)
232	ed. (Unto ... tongue / Satisfie ... longing Q1)
234	ed. (Is ... thee / Tell ... this Q1)
238	ed. (I'll know / Will ... me / No ... shall Q1)
241	ed. (The ... folly / But ...tyranny Q1)
244	ed. (May ... of / Therefore ... it Q1)
248	ed. (Till ... you / You'll ... it / Never Q1)
258	ed. (Now ... me / No ... it Q1)
261	ed. (Were strangled / Oh ... done Q1)
264–6	ed. (For ... secret / You ... sir / Why / It ... it / No... booke Q1)
271–2	ed. (I ... death / For ... hold / Ha *Bosola* / I ... you Q1)
276–7	ed. (It ... it. / Oh ... woman / Couldst ... him / Tis weakenesse Q1)
283	ed. (To ... seruice / I'll ... peeces Q1)
286	ed. (Who ... here / Her ... intended Q1)
303	ed. (Yes / Take ... body / I ... shall Q)
306	ed. (To ... murther / Oh ... meanes Q1)
307–13	prose ed. (*Q1 lines ending* swelling / them / blood / Gallowes / body / Plague / death)*
315	ed. (He's ... possession / Of ... Citadell Q1)
319	ed. (What ... you / You ... ready Q1)

V.iii

9	ed. (That ... answeres / I ... ruynes Q1)
19	ed. (Must ... have / Like ... *haue* Q1)
20	ed. (Now ... you / It ... gaue Q1)
21	ed. (A ... Accent / *Deadly Accent* Q1)
24	ed. (Or ... Sorrow / *A ... Sorrow* Q1)
25	ed. (I ... best / *That ... best* Q1)
26	ed. ('Tis ... voyce / *Ay ... –voyce* Q1)
29	ed. (Doe not / *Doe not* Q1)
32	ed. (*Be ... safety* / Necessitie compells me Q1)
35	ed. (To ... fate / *O ... fate* Q1)
39	ed. (For ... Thing / *Thou ... Thing* Q1)
42	ed. (Shall ... more / *Never ... more* Q1)
46	ed. (Your ... meerely / Come ... Ague Q1)
50	ed. (Loose ... nothing / Your ... you Q1)
54	ed. (The ... compassion / How ... well Q1)

V.iv

3	ed. (Good ... vs / Oh ... meanes Q1)
7	ed. (Do ... you / So ... not Q1)
12	ed. (Nor ... followers / Neither Q1)
16	ed. (And ... danger / If ... cutting Q1)
18	ed. (Why ... you / 'Twas ... night Q1)

25–6 ed. (*one line* Q1)*
45 ed. (There ... pardon / Fall ... sword Q1)
48 ed. (In ... mynut / What ... thou / A ... thing Q1)
50 ed. (To ... selfe / Where ... Sir Q1)
51 ed. (Very ... *Bosola* / Oh. .. misfortune Q1)
58–9 ed. (And ... Children / Their ... names / Kindle ... me / Are murderd Q1)
71 ed. (To Delio / Breake heart Q1)
73 ed. (Thou ... *Antonio* / I ... hether Q1)

V.v

10–12 ed. (Mixed ... feare / Thus ... Action / I ... thee / Hah ... Guard / Thou ... deceiu'd / They ... howling Q1)*
14–16 ed. (Revenewes ... thee / Thy ... proffers / Are ... vnseasonable / Raise ... betraid / I ... flight Q1)
18 ed. (But ... further / Help ... betraid / Listen Q1)
19 ed. (My ... rescew / Fye ... counterfeyting Q1)
20 ed. (Why ... Cardinall / Yes ... he Q1)
23 ed. (Unless ...rescew / He ... well Q1)
25 ed. (The ... throat / You ... then Q1)
30 ed. (Force ... doores / Let's ... aloofe Q1)
32–5 ed. (There's ... doore / To ... rescew / What ... life / Looke there Q1)*
36 ed. (*Antonio* / Slaine ... vnwittingly Q1)
39 ed. (And ... sword / O ... mercy Q1)
43 ed. (Thou ... me / Againe / Shall ... Levoret Q1)
50 ed. (Help ... brother / The diuell Q1)
51 ed. (There ... ransome / Oh ... Justice Q1)
56–61 prose ed. (*Q1 lines ending* fellowes / *Pompey's* / prosperity / field / with / sight / you)*
68–9 ed. (Beyond death / He ... bottom Q1)*
79 ed. (How ... Lord / Oh ... disastre / How ... this Q1)
86 ed. (Neglected / How ... Lord / Look ... brother Q1)
91 ed. (His ... rescew / Thou ... blood Q1)
108 ed. (Oh ... late / I ... and Q1)